*2 – To Roanne,*

*Enjoy reading,*

*Ben Meyer*

# A YEAR of SPIRITUAL COMPANIONSHIP

## 52 WEEKS OF WISDOM FOR A LIFE OF GRATITUDE, BALANCE AND HAPPINESS

ANNE KERTZ KERNION

FOREWORD BY
REV. CAROL HOWARD MERRITT

*Walking Together, Finding the Way*®

**SKYLIGHT PATHS**®
PUBLISHING

Woodstock, Vermont

*A Year of Spiritual Companionship:*
*52 Weeks of Wisdom for a Life of Gratitude, Balance and Happiness*

2016 Quality Paperback Edition, Second Printing
© 2016 by Anne Kertz Kernion
Foreword © 2016 by Carol Howard Merritt

**Library of Congress Cataloging-in-Publication Data**
Names: Kernion, Anne Kertz, 1958– author.
Title: A year of spiritual companionship : 52 weeks of wisdom for a life of gratitude, balance and happiness / Anne Kertz Kernion.
Description: Quality Paperback Edition. | Woodstock, VT : SkyLight Paths Publishing, 2016. | Includes bibliographical references.
Identifiers: LCCN 2015043251| ISBN 9781594736179 (pbk.) | ISBN 9781594736285 (ebook)
Subjects: LCSH: Spiritual life. | Spiritual exercises. | Conduct of life.
Classification: LCC BL624 .K468 2016 | DDC 204/.32—dc23
LC record available at http://lccn.loc.gov/2015043251.

10 9 8 7 6 5 4 3 2

Manufactured in the United States of America
Cover design: Jenny Buono
Interior design: Tim Holtz
Cover art: Anne Kertz Kernion

SkyLight Paths, "Walking Together, Finding the Way" and colophon are trademarks of LongHill Partners, Inc., registered in the U.S. Patent and Trademark Office.

*Walking Together, Finding the Way*
Published by SkyLight Paths Publishing
A Division of LongHill Partners, Inc.
Sunset Farm Offices, Route 4, P.O. Box 237
Woodstock, VT 05091
Tel: (802) 457-4000   Fax: (802) 457-4004
www.skylightpaths.com

For Jack

"If I know what love is,
it is because of you."
—Herman Hesse

# CONTENTS

# FOREWORD

My phone buzzes from the bedside table, jarring me from needed sleep. Blurry-eyed, I look down at the email notification and wonder why I never took the time to learn how to put my phone to sleep. Now that it vibrates and glows next to me like a pet needing food and affection, something in my core jumps to attention, ready to respond, even though my exhausted extremities yearn to stay in bed. When my eyes focus on the text, it reminds me of something very important that slipped between the cracks yesterday.

I peel the sheets off, make coffee, and begin my workday. I usually start toiling from my couch, in my bathrobe, before the sun rises. I'm a writer, so the wee hours prove most productive. Words pour easily when I can hear the hushed hum of the refrigerator and intuit sleeping breaths of my family. So I open my laptop and respond to that email. It takes a while, because I have to research some information. It also reminds me of another email I have to answer, so I attend to it. Yet another email rolls in, and just as I'm about done replying to it, I think about how so many people do work on other forms of social media. So I check all of my direct messages and private messages, to be sure I answer everything on those pages.

Soon, my attention has been scattered to the winds. I feel the forces whipping around me, as I fetch this report and work on that assignment. Someone needs a favor, and another person would like a book recommendation. I must write an article, attend a conference call, and the emails never stop. Hours pass, with all of my energy and creativity directed and guided by the force of conflicting gales. Before I know it, my workday is over. Eight hours have passed, and I have been thrashing around, carrying out other people's agendas.

I suppose this would be okay, if my job was being part of a support staff and I needed to be attentive to everyone else's needs. But it's not. I'm a writer, who must stay rooted and grounded to her vocation in order to put words on a page. And now I'm realizing that I've had too many days caught up in this windstorm.

In the midst of this tug and pull of my day, I pick up the wise and gentle words of Anne Kertz Kernion, and she takes up the journey alongside me. *A Year of Spiritual Companionship* doesn't distract me with more outside gusts or diversions. It doesn't come at me as a self-help list of things I ought to be doing, adding to my full life, but focuses me on my own path. Each week offers practices that encourage gratitude, mindfulness, and listening. The words offer wise advice from mystics and enlightening science from neuroscientists, and as we continue our journey together, I become aware of the firm ground supporting, sweet air sustaining, and savory food nourishing me. The tornado settles and I am reminded, once again, how to be human.

With gratitude for Anne's words, I hand this book over to you, so that we might journey, contemplate, and practice together.

Rev. Carol Howard Merritt

# INTRODUCTION

> Listen to your life. See it for the fathomless
> mystery it is. In the boredom and pain of it, no
> less than in the excitement and gladness: touch,
> taste, smell your way to the holy and hidden heart
> of it, because in the last analysis all moments
> are key moments, and life itself is grace.
>
> —FREDERICK BUECHNER

This book is designed to be a companion for your spiritual journey, a week-by-week guide to living more thoughtfully. Whether you are just beginning to explore your path or you've been journeying for decades, the reflections and practices here are meant to encourage and inspire. They remind you how to bring peace, connection, and heartfelt living to your everyday busy life. In these pages, you will discover—or perhaps rediscover—spiritual practices such as mindfulness and gratitude that have proven to enrich the lives of practitioners through the ages. In addition, current research by neuroscientists and psychologists provides you with insights that can improve not only your mental and spiritual health but also your physical well-being.

I grew up surrounded almost exclusively by Catholics. Until I was twelve years old, I thought that kids who attended public school belonged to a religion named "Public." When I learned in high school that there were other religions that had helpful insights into spirituality, this was big news. My world religions class readings affirmed my contemplative leanings and launched me into a lifelong quest of spiritual discovery. Even as I studied environmental engineering in college, I read many books on spirituality in my free time.

After graduation, I worked in engineering but left after only two years in the workforce to pursue a master's degree in theology, where the topics matched my deepest interests. In the process, I discovered the wonderful commonalities shared by science and theology. In addition to teaching us to think clearly, both disciplines discuss how values such as connection and gratitude are important to our physical and spiritual health. Groundbreaking research in neuroscience and psychology often corresponds to what spiritual sages have taught for many centuries.

Another longtime interest of mine has been collecting quotations. Since I was a little girl, quotations have touched my heart, encouraged me, and admonished me to be more compassionate and understanding. They were the basis for launching my greeting card company over thirty years ago. You'll find many of my favorite quotations scattered throughout the following pages.

So this book is the story of lessons I've learned on my circuitous spiritual journey. Some lessons come directly through the wisdom of spiritual luminaries and other significant people in my life, some from the process of running a small business, and some from reading neuroscience, psychology, sociology, and spirituality. Some lessons have been easy to learn; some have taken years to seep into my bones; and others are going to take a lifetime of practice.

While all this wisdom and guidance is important and needed, not all of it is groundbreaking or new. I assume much of what you read here will be familiar. And some of the spiritual themes and practices are revisited over the months because we all need the reminders. One mention of the need to express gratitude, no matter how much inspiration it sparks at the time, will soon be swallowed up by all the information we take in throughout each day.

One of the big keys to the spiritual life is remembering. We remember to be aware in each moment, and then we forget. We remember to be grateful every day, and then we forget. We remember to be compassionate with ourselves, and then we forget. So I've included some practical tips at the end of each week's reflection to help you remember and bring that wisdom into your everyday life. At the end of the year, you'll have tried many different practices and hopefully found a few you connect with and can practice for years to come.

The weekly lessons here can be used alone or with a group of fellow seekers. Each month has four entries, with four bonus entries at the end to comprise fifty-two weeks. If a month has more than four weeks, you can choose one of these additional lessons for your weekly inspiration.

Years ago, I taught a course in religious meaning and spirituality at a local college. Occasionally, a student would balk at my pronouncement that each person in the room had a spirituality.

So I would ask the student how she lived out the truths in her life. What did she care about most intensely and how did she express that? Where did she most come alive? In answering, she would discover her deepest beliefs, what I would name her "spirituality." The class readings and discussions would help her realize how she could be in touch with that spirituality and live those truths more regularly. In this book I try to do the same, by exploring dimensions of spirituality and the ways we can live out our "truths" more deeply and consistently. I would be honored to have you join me in the journey. As Robert Muller, former United Nations diplomat, noted, "All we can do is put our full love into our lives ... making a work of art of the precious years that are granted to us."

# JANUARY

## Week One

It's never too late to be who you might have been.
—GEORGE ELIOT (MARY ANN EVANS)

And suddenly you know: it's time to start something
new and trust the magic of beginnings.
—MEISTER ECKHART

We enter a new year, called to begin again. We might
make a resolution or two, hoping to modify a habit or
perhaps start practicing a new one. But as we all know, trying
to transform our behavior and loosen a habit's grip on us is
easier said than done. If you've made a resolution to change,
you've already taken the most important step. Congratulations!

You might ask what habits have to do with our spirituality.
I would argue, everything! Philosopher William James astutely
observed, "All our life ... is but a mass of habits." Aristotle
noted that the behaviors we do unthinkingly are the evidence
of our truest selves. I'm not encouraging perfection—a certain

path to discouragement and derailment—yet there are small steps we can take to bring out the best in ourselves, and the first place to begin is an examination of our habits.

Perhaps we want to make more time for prayer, contemplation, or meditation; more time to develop our unique gifts and serve others with them, to be present to our loved ones; more time to exercise and prepare healthy meals. Perhaps we want to stop being so judgmental or critical of others, to listen more and talk less. Or perhaps we hope to be more tender and softhearted. If we don't examine our everyday behaviors once in a while, behaviors that one by one add up to our habits, we aren't making room for the growth and change we desire. So to begin this new year, let's look at our habits and see if they aid our spiritual growth or hinder it.

We frequently talk about habits in a disparaging way, but habits are an essential part of our daily functioning. We can't possibly think carefully about every single action we take each and every day. We need habits to allow our brains the space to do the hard stuff. It's not easy to nurture the good ones and eliminate the bad ones, and we won't be perfect, but the effort is important and change is possible.

Pulitzer Prize–winning reporter Charles Duhigg, in his book *The Power of Habit*, shows us how to alter the patterns that shape our daily lives. Our habits determine the quality of our day-to-day existence, what we will accomplish in the years we have here on earth, and whether we are happy and fulfilled or sad and discouraged. Duhigg explains the science behind those daily actions and then helps us figure out how to focus on the correct measures so we maximize our innate abilities.

The first step toward establishing a new habit is finding a simple and obvious "instigation cue." This means that you can turn habits into automatic decisions prompted by your own internal or environmental cues. For example, you might want to begin walking every morning before work. A simple cue would be to have your clothes and shoes ready the night before, placed next to your bed. Now all you have to do is wake up, get into your clothes, and walk out the door. You don't say to yourself, *Do I really want to do this? Maybe thirty minutes more of sleep would be better today.* You don't need to do anything but follow the cues you've established.

According to a study of exercise habits at Iowa State University, the only factor that predicts how often a person will exercise over the long term is the strength of his or her instigation cue. So whether your new habit involves exercise or not, having a cue will be one of the most important steps in cementing that habit for the long run.

# Putting the Wisdom into Practice

Choose one habit you'd like to nourish this month, one that might allow your spirituality to grow and deepen. What instigation cue could help you get started? Maybe showering or drinking tea or coffee in the morning can be the cue to take five deep breaths in gratitude. If you'd like to bring more prayer time into your life, perhaps you can place a candle, cushion

or chair, and inspirational book in a corner of a room. Now
you're ready to sit and spend some quiet moments there each
morning before starting your day. Set your alarm for just two to
five minutes earlier. Starting small ensures that you can build
it into your life easily. (Who can argue that we don't have an
extra two minutes each day?) Good luck! We'll check back on
our habit-building process in two weeks.

# Week Two

When asked if my cup is half-full or half-empty, my only response is that I am thankful I have a cup.

—SAM LEFKOWITZ

It is only with gratitude that life becomes rich.

—DIETRICH BONHOEFFER

One habit that has had a significant impact on my life is the practice of gratitude. Cultivating gratitude has generated joy at times I wouldn't expect it.

What exactly is gratitude? It is:

- Wonder
- Appreciation
- Looking on the bright side
- Thanking someone
- Being aware of abundance
- Thanking God
- Counting our blessings
- Savoring (not rushing forward)
- Not taking things for granted

What is *not* gratitude? It is not comparing, for starters. If we are in the habit of comparing ourselves to others, constantly asking ourselves, *What does Susie have that I don't have?*—a better job, health, house, car, wardrobe, family, life situation—then we are never satisfied. We might even compare our current selves to our younger selves—I used to have fewer wrinkles and more energy, more fun and less anxiety, thicker hair and a thinner body. But when we practice gratitude, we focus on being grateful for *this*, so we don't need to long for *that*.

Gratitude also opens our eyes to the gifts all around us. Catholic theologian Henri Nouwen explains, "Gratitude involves a conscious choice. I can choose to be grateful even when my emotions and feelings are steeped in hurt and resentment.… I can choose gratitude instead of a complaint."

Gratitude takes the little—and big—inconveniences and disruptions of life and makes me aware of the blessings inside those experiences. When I find myself suffering due to an exercise-related injury, for example, I take stock and give thanks for the fact that I *can* still ride my bike or do yoga most days. Giving thanks for what I *can* do instead of what I *can't* makes the day much better.

Benedictine monk Brother David Steindl-Rast, the preeminent teacher on gratitude, has devoted his life to sharing the practice of gratefulness. He recommends trying to find a new thing to be grateful for every day, advising:

> Pay attention each day to one smell, one sound which we never appreciated before, to one color or shape, one texture, one taste to which we never before paid attention. Dedicate one day each week to a different sense.[1]

Several recent scientific studies by Dr. Robert Emmons, Dr. Martin Seligman, and other social scientists conclude that gratitude has many physical and psychological benefits. These include stronger immune systems, increased sleep quality, lower blood pressure, better exercise patterns, higher levels of positive emotions, more compassion and generous actions, and feeling less lonely and isolated.

Gratitude also staves off what is known as "hedonic adaptation." This refers to the way we get accustomed to the good things that come our way: the new car, new house, new job, new relationship. We are excited and happy at first, but once we adapt to our new situation, we often begin to take it for granted. Dr. Seligman reminds us that if we can remember to be grateful for these new circumstances, we keep the awareness of our blessings at the forefront and become happier as a result.

The more we remember to live in a state of gratitude, the better we feel and the more motivated we are to continue practicing gratitude. The tricky part is remembering. We have to keep up the practice of "looking for the good" in every single day. That's why habits are key to developing an attitude of gratitude.

# Putting the Wisdom into Practice

1. Keep a "What Went Well" journal: Write down what went well every day, or even just once a week. Name three different things each time you write.
2. Be present. Be grateful. When engaged in a "boring" task—doing dishes, taking out the trash, folding laundry, watering plants—breathe and be grateful instead of wishing you were doing something else.

3. Express gratitude to others. Every day, thank someone: your partner, friend, or coworker for their presence, their gifts, their goodness. You can do this verbally, in an email, or in a handwritten note. (I advocate for the latter!)

4. Take time for silence. By pausing, we create the space to be aware of the gifts showering down upon us all day long.

# Week Three

> Gratitude unlocks the fullness of life. It turns what we have into enough, and more. It can turn a meal into a feast, a house into a home, a stranger into a friend.
>
> —MELODY BEATTIE

> Keep fresh before me the moments of my high resolve.
>
> —HOWARD THURMAN

Now that we've entered the third week of the year, it's time to revisit our plan for habit change and see what other aids we can discover to help us keep our intentions alive. It isn't enough just to hope for change. If that were all that was necessary, not one of us would fail to keep our New Year's resolutions. But most of us find that by the end of January, many of our resolutions have derailed. We need determination, commitment, and a plan to follow in order to keep on track—or get back on track. Remember that the first step in creating new habits is setting the cue. The second step is clearly defining the reward that's coming and triggering a craving for that reward. So if we consider a walking habit, the reward could be the sense of satisfaction and enjoyment of the quiet time. Or the gratification of knowing we've burned calories and helped our heart and lungs stay healthy. Whatever we think of as our reward, it's important to take time to ponder it and establish a yearning for it.

Habits are powerful because they create these neurological cravings. For example, I crave the endorphins and the sense of accomplishment I experience every time I finish a workout, whether it's bike riding or yoga or hiking. On some days when I'm not the least bit motivated to exercise, I just think of how good I'll feel when I'm finished. Usually that's enough to get me out the door. Recent studies show that the more immediate the reward, the more we crave it and are motivated to continue doing the activity.

William James writes that habits allow us to "do a thing with difficulty the first time, but soon do it more and more easily, and finally, with sufficient practice, do it semi-mechanically, or with hardly any consciousness at all." People grow "to the way in which they have been exercised."

"Keystone habits" are habits that matter more than others. They start a process that, after a while, transforms everything we do. They encourage new values and goals that, once ingrained, change our entire decision-making process. For example, something about getting into the habit of exercising transforms other areas of our lives: we eat healthier, produce more quality work, smoke less, are more patient, and feel less stress. Being an exerciser makes other good habits easier to cultivate.

Many studies show that willpower is the single most important keystone habit for individual success. Forget intellectual talent. If a person has good self-regulating skills, she will be a success. The more you practice distracting yourself from temptations, the easier it is to regulate your impulses. It becomes second nature to forgo that donut or slice of pie if you've practiced doing so over and over again.

# Putting the Wisdom into Practice

Have you been able to consistently practice the new habit you started at the beginning of the year? It'll help your determination if you identify a reward associated with the new habit and establish a craving for it. The more you embed that craving in your mind, the easier it is to stick with the new routine.

If you're still struggling to firmly root your habit, perhaps it would help if you asked a friend to join you. Then you can hold each other accountable to reach your goals.

# Week Four

No success, however glittering, that denies
yourself will make you happy in the long run.
So listen to the voice from your soul, quiet but
insistent, and honor it. Find what you thrill to.

—ROGER COHEN

The happiness of your life depends upon the quality
of your thoughts: therefore, guard accordingly.

—MARCUS AURELIUS

I n January we celebrate the feast day of Brother Lawrence, who lived as a monk in seventeenth-century France. Although crippled and in chronic pain, and assigned the most mundane jobs in his monastery's kitchen, he was known as a gentle man with a joyful spirit. How could he be so content with his boring and tedious life? Did he discover what sixteenth-century Christian mystic Teresa of Ávila meant when she proclaimed, "The Lord is found amidst the pots and pans"? Do these two—and others like them—know something about happiness that might help us modern folk live with greater joy?

Happiness is multifaceted, as psychology professor Sonja Lyubomirsky reports in *The How of Happiness*. She found that 40 percent of our happiness is determined by how we act and think. The rest of our happiness is dependent upon our genetically determined set point (50 percent) and life circumstances (10 percent). So what actions and thoughts can boost our happiness?

First, happy people nurture their relationships, sharing joys, sorrows, lives. Those who have the best relationships are people who are happy for others when they have *good* news. So while it's crucial to support friends and loved ones when they're struggling, it's also important to rejoice when they experience good fortune. (Check that jealousy at the door!) The happier we can be for others, the happier we will be ourselves.

Second, we can increase our day-to-day happiness by practicing kindness, at least once a week and in a variety of ways. Hold a door for someone, send a thoughtful note, bake cookies to share, lend an ear to a friend, help a neighbor with yard work—the list is endless. The neuroscience research of professor Richard Davidson shows that the best way to be happy is to be generous toward others. Not that we help others solely to make us feel good, but the goodness overflows to all.

Third, practice gratitude. Brother David Steindl-Rast advises us to be grateful *in* a situation, not necessarily *for* a situation. For example, I undergo colonoscopies every five years. The preparation the day before is terribly unpleasant. But instead of complaining about it, I could focus on being grateful that these lifesaving tests exist and are covered by my health insurance.

Fourth, savor all of life and live in the present. Try spending less time mulling over the past and worrying about the future. I know, it's not easy. But by staying firmly grounded in the present, we can more easily relish the ordinary experiences of everyday life. Mihaly Csikszentmihalyi, author of *Flow: The Psychology of Optimal Experience*, found that we are happiest when we are in the state of "flow," where we are completely absorbed in an activity that balances our skills and the challenges of the activity. Time drops away and we are engaged and immersed, and our whole being is involved in using our skills. The more "flow" we create in our lives, the happier we will be.

Fifth, think about your lifelong goals and dreams and work toward them every day. Lyubomirsky says, "Find a happy person and you will find a project." Our projects don't have to be big and important, but they should be something we're passionate about, something that gets our hearts pumping and our minds engaged.

Sixth, don't let your mind tell you that you're "too old" to do something. I have a great role model in my eighty-seven-year-old dad. He continues to work every day in the business he founded in 1947. He still mows the grass, rakes the leaves, and occasionally shoots at the squirrels in his yard. Dad embodies what Harvard researcher Ellen Langer has confirmed in her studies: our attitudes about aging will support or undermine the quality of our later years. She has found clear links between what our minds *think* we can do, and what we *can* do. In her 1979 "Counterclockwise" study, which she discusses in her book *Mindfulness*, she re-created the social and physical environment of 1959 for eight elderly men. After one week at this residential retreat setting, living as though it were twenty years ago, all eight participants showed marked improvements in their hearing, memory, dexterity, strength, and general well-being.

And finally, care for body and soul. Get enough sleep. Find a way to exercise that's enjoyable to you. Nurture your soul by joining a prayer or study group. Caring for our spirits is an integral part of living a happy, meaningful life. One of my favorite ways of grounding my soul in the wintertime is snowshoeing. I head out to a nearby trail through the woods and spend an hour trudging through the snow, observing the trees, sky, snow, brush, branches with a few leftover berries, and occasional bird. I come home a "softer Anne," wrapped in a blanket of peace, awareness, and happiness.

# Putting the Wisdom into Practice

Try one of these happiness practices this week. Then try another one. If you work several of these activities into your days, you'll find more joy visiting you and everyone around you. Our beacons can shine a little brighter in our corner of the world.

# FEBRUARY

 Week One

Through love, through friendship,
a heart lives more than once.

—ANAÏS NIN

I have never met a person whose greatest need was
anything other than real, unconditional love.

—ELISABETH KÜBLER-ROSS

We celebrate the heart this month. We ponder love and maybe even send a Valentine or two to loved ones. My husband, Jack, and I were married in the month of February, so we especially celebrate love during this month. The Dutch priest who married us, Father John Fonville, was a dear friend of Jack's before we met, and I grew to love him as well. Father John spent months preparing the homily for our wedding, drawing upon his extensive knowledge of world literature to compose some of the most beautiful reflections on marriage I have ever heard. Here are some of my favorite passages:

Anne and Jack, paradise on earth beckons you, and the gate to it is true love.

Jack, you are to love Anne truly. That's what she expects but that is also what she needs to blossom and grow into the heart you want her to become and remain; your own pulsating heart, the heart of your beginning family. Your hand must remove the stones on her path. Your words of compliment and love must fall every day, every day, like flowers on the road you travel together. And your eyes, those windows of your soul, must convey your affection and guard the smile on her lips and the laughter in her eyes. Because when they fade away and die, true love will have been killed. True love is you, and you always, and you only, the art of all arts, the great art of true love.

Anne, you must love Jack with all your body, with all your mind, with all your heart, and with all your soul. You'll make him so rich and happy that he has a taste of heaven on earth. He'll kiss the ground you travel....

True love, Anne and Jack, is so full of trust that there is no opening for doubt, so full of forgiveness that there is always willingness to excuse, to pardon and accept human deficiency and frailty, so faithful that the emotions which flowered in you are preserved in higher aims. Then the lovable each saw in the other will not crumble in time, but still be recognizable in the bent figure and the silver hair.

May I end this homily on your sweet, glorious day with a prayer ...

O God, protect the love of all lovers. You know how fragile and almost nothing are two humans and that a heart is restless and changeable like the weather. You have turned them toward one another that they may not be half anymore and unfulfilled. Teach them the terrifying secret that to love is to suffer. But also that to give is truly living. Give them time to know one another. May they be so intimately united that when one weeps the other will taste salt.

Nothing great in this world is ever accomplished without true passion. And so we ask God to guide and also increase the fire of their genuine passion. May they never be healed from the gentle wound of true love. Make them patient and infinitely tender with one another that they may spend their days, their nights, time and eternity together. Amen, so be it. Yes, amen.

# Putting the Wisdom into Practice

One practice that increases our happiness, as we saw in January, is nurturing relationships. We have the perfect opportunity to open our hearts to others in this month. Valentine's Day may have been hijacked by consumerism, but its original intention of love and goodwill can still guide our actions. Buy or make a few cards—or write a quick email or text message—and send them to your favorite people. There isn't a person alive who wouldn't be glad to be reminded of someone's love for them.

# Week Two

Earth's crammed with heaven,
And every common bush afire with God,
But only he who sees takes off his shoes ...
—ELIZABETH BARRETT BROWNING

Delight in simple things.
—RUDYARD KIPLING

The task of observing things and people around us with a set of fresh eyes—to let go of our preconceptions and be amazed by a first impression again—is certainly a spiritual exercise worthy of our best efforts. If we are in too much of a hurry, we miss wonderful moments of grace, wonder, and joy. As English mystic Evelyn Underhill wrote, "For lack of attention, a thousand forms of loveliness elude us every day."

When we watch small children discover the world, we experience the familiar in a new way, encountering it all afresh through their eyes and ears. We cease the rushing, which is a gift in itself, and observe what grabs their attention. (And hope sometimes it's us!) Their excitement with the unfamiliar brings joy aplenty to our lives.

Our family has welcomed three grandchildren in recent years, and we've discovered the undeniable truth that young children delight in the tiniest of things. Our grandson, Percy, is a naturally happy and effervescent child. A few weeks after his birth, while playing the role of "grandma-in-residence," I took him on walks when he grew restless. Luckily for us, the narrow walkway outside his parents' apartment was lined with a wide variety of trees, and Percy's attention was instantly drawn to them. He was content to just gaze at the leaves and branches for several minutes at a time. As I held his face near the big leaves and flowers he would coo and become perfectly satisfied.

These marvelous little babies come into the world already knowing how to savor. It's innate for them, since everything in their world is a fresh discovery. They teach us what it means to appreciate, to take in the world with new eyes, and to delight in all the simple things.

The happiest people I know savor life's joys and delight in simple pleasures. They appreciate what life has to offer and refrain from dwelling on the past or fretting over the future. They attend to the moment, live mindfully in the present, and are full of gratitude for life. They anticipate the future, but also relish the small gifts that each day may bring: stopping to watch the sunset, gazing at the full moon overhead, lingering over warm coffee or tea in the morning, enveloping a child in a hug. With their lives, they teach us: *Enjoy the little things, for one day we'll look back and realize that these were, in fact, the big things.*

## Putting the Wisdom into Practice

If you have small children in your life, spend a few moments observing how they encounter the world. Take an hour or two to live at their pace, seeing everything through their eyes. Watch how they investigate and experience new things. Use them to model your actions this week. "Take off your shoes," as Elizabeth Barrett Browning suggests.

Stop a few times a day to pause and appreciate. Look at the familiar faces around you and recall what you love most about them.

# Week Three

Holiness isn't something ephemeral or amorphous that exists out there in the heavens. Holiness is what occurs when any of us chooses to be fully present to another.

—LEAF SELIGMAN

Holy listening—to "listen" another's soul into life ... may be the greatest service that any human being ever performs for another.

—DOUGLAS STEERE

Listening is an essential spiritual practice. When we listen, we become aware of the natural wonders around us. We become present and attentive to others, and open to their wisdom. We hear what others are communicating, both verbally and nonverbally, and can discern the best way to serve and love them. We are able to capture the important lessons that spiritual and sacred texts provide.

Listening can be done anywhere: in a waiting room, on the elevator, at the post office, on the bus, in the grocery store, at a cocktail party or a meeting. It's not always easy, but it's a tangible gift we can give to others. It also takes humility to listen, because we are stopping what we are doing and, in effect, saying, "You're more important than my to-do list." But looking away when someone is talking to you shouts, "I don't care about you ... I can't even give you eye contact!"

Here's one of my favorite stories illustrating "holy listening":

> A man whose marriage was in trouble sought the advice of a teacher, who said: "You must learn to listen to your wife."
>
> The man took this advice to heart and returned after a month to report that he had learned to listen to every word his wife was saying.
>
> Said the teacher with a smile, "Now go home and listen to every word she isn't saying."

People communicate plenty with their body language and tone of voice. This is particularly important to keep in mind with those who are hurting or struggling. We often say, "Let me know if you need anything." But people usually don't let us know, so we need to listen in other, less verbal, ways.

In his column titled "The Art of Presence," *New York Times* writer David Brooks offered some wise words of counsel when a friend, neighbor, or family member faces a loss.

1. Be there. Show up. You can't fix things, but you can walk through the pain with them. Assume people need presence.

2. Don't compare. Ever. Each loss or trauma is different. Resist the urge to say things like, "I know what you're feeling. I lost my _____." That is not helpful.

3. See what is needed and bring it. Don't ask. Just do it. The recipients will be grateful.

4. Do not say, "You'll get over it." No one gets over a great loss.

5. Keep checking in. They are still in need of your presence and care a few weeks or months later.

6. Don't say, "It's all for the best," or try to make sense out of what happened. Just say, "I'm so sorry."[1]

We are made to connect with one another, to help each other on our journeys, particularly when things are difficult. Our gift of listening allows us to discern what is needed. We then can offer our love and encouragement in response, through our physical presence, our sensitivity, and our thoughtful deeds. As Henri Nouwen says, "The friend who can be silent with us in a moment of despair or confusion, who can stay with us in an hour of grief and bereavement, who can tolerate not knowing, not curing, not healing and face with us the reality of our powerlessness, that is a friend who cares."

# Putting the Wisdom into Practice

Bring your presence and holy listening skills to your conversations this week. Try speaking half as much as you listen. Take time to listen fully, with your whole being. Remember to bring an extra dose of humility to your encounters. At the end of each day, ponder those experiences and what you might have learned from them. Continue honing your listening skills as you move through the week.

If you know someone who has recently suffered a loss, find out what they most need and deliver it to them. If you aren't sure, just send a thoughtful note or a dessert to let them know they are in your thoughts and are not alone.

# Week Four

The thing that is really hard, and really
amazing, is giving up on being perfect and
beginning the work of becoming yourself.

—ANNA QUINDLEN

Accept yourself just as you are ... your faults and
limitations. Recognize them and be with them,
without trying to correct them directly. As you
watch them, feel them, and accept them, their
force and exaggeration will gradually diminish.

—FATHER THOMAS KEATING

Several classrooms in my Catholic grade school had a poster
that read, "God does not make junk." (I remember thinking to myself, *Of course not!*) Another phrase I heard frequently
was, "Love your neighbor as yourself." Our teachers correctly
pointed out that the "love ourselves" part was sometimes over-
shadowed by the "neighbor" part. I knew I should love myself,
but not until I was much older did I realize how complicated
that was.

In *The Gifts of Imperfection,* research professor Brené Brown
shows us how we can learn to accept ourselves, *love* ourselves,
even with our many flaws. For a recovering perfectionist like
me, it was a powerful read. I need to practice self-acceptance
every day, because I easily slip into thinking, *I can't make a*

*mistake because then no one will like me/think I'm worthy* ... Silly. I know. But it's the truth. So perhaps you'll find some of Brown's suggestions helpful, as I have:

1. We connect most deeply with others through our *imperfections*. Perfectionism is found, in varying degrees, in most humans. We twist ourselves in knots, doing things to gain approval and love. Sound familiar? (That's me with my hand up!) Boy, it would be so healthy for all of us if we could let go of what people think and accept ourselves, bumps and warts and all. I know, it's really hard to do. We need to let go of the need to look perfect and relax into who we are. Then we'll nourish a deep closeness with other human beings.

2. Let's stop holding ourselves to ridiculously high standards in a quest to prove our worth to others. If you use social media frequently, you may think everyone else has a perfect life. Think again. That's usually just the veneer people project to the world. Virginia Woolf remarked, "No need to hurry. No need to sparkle. No need to be anyone but yourself." We are already enough.

3. Let's be gentle and compassionate with ourselves, particularly when we make mistakes. No one is perfect. Compassion toward ourselves leads to compassion toward others. We often give others the benefit of the doubt much more readily than we give it to ourselves.

When we are our authentic selves, we wind up connecting to others at a deeper level. Don't we love the company of folks who are "real" and comfortable in their own skin? Recently, I've been practicing being real with my yoga class. Sometimes I lose track of which pose comes next and ask the class for help, creating a collaborative atmosphere. Sometimes I'm not able to fully demonstrate a pose due to tight hips or an injured knee, giving everyone permission to accept their limitations, too. We acknowledge our imperfections without judging ourselves or each other, creating a more caring, honest, and nurturing environment.

## Putting the Wisdom into Practice

Begin to notice how perfectionism creeps into your day. Are you trying to gain approval from another instead of simply being who you are? In your conversations with others, be honest about who you are, what you can and cannot do. When you make a mistake, acknowledge it and move on. Stop beating yourself up about being a human being who has flaws. We all do! Treat yourself with the kindness that you show your friends.

# MARCH

# Week One

What a person takes in by contemplation,
he pours out in love.

It is in deep solitude that I find the gentleness
with which I can truly love others.

The season of Lent is a sacred time of reflection and spiritual growth for Christians around the world. A religious sister friend of mine calls it "the time to practice who we want to become." I like that outlook because it acknowledges the open-ended nature of the journey. We will never be perfect, but we can try to be more thoughtful, compassionate, and kind. Lent is a season set aside to reflect on our spiritual journeys, a time to make adjustments to our trajectories, a time to pay attention to our attitudes and actions.

The Benedictine tradition offers several nuggets of wisdom to inspire us on this forty-day journey. St. Benedict reminds us to be attentive, to listen carefully to one another, and to have mutual respect and concern for all human beings. Humility, he says, is what keeps us real. We don't overestimate our strengths, but recognize what gifts we have and use them to serve others. He challenges us to a conversion of manners: he asks us to evaluate not what we do but the way we perform our daily tasks.

This last piece of advice reminds me of a story told about the Trappist monk Thomas Merton. On a visit to another monastery, he asked one of the novices what he had learned during his first year of living as a monk. Expecting to hear stories of enlightenment and discoveries of the spirit, what he heard instead was, "I learned to open and close doors."

The way we open and close doors indicates whether or not we are attentive, aware of the moment, aware of others, and aware of God's presence. Each act of opening or closing a door can remind us to pay attention to the way we are living. This simple exercise can help us practice who we want to become: people who are loving, kind, and considerate. It might also remind us to take a few moments of solitude to nurture our compassion for ourselves.

## Putting the Wisdom into Practice

This week, bring your awareness to every door you open or close. You'll probably be surprised by how many there are:

every cupboard and cabinet door, every closet and room of your home, every outside entrance. Allow that awareness of each opening and closing to bring you back to the present moment. Check in with yourself and ask, *How am I doing? Am I practicing patience and understanding, or am I being self-centered and irritated by the demands of the day?* By the end of the week, you'll have learned to open and close doors like the young monk: with attention, thought, and care.

# Week Two

I want first of all to be at peace with myself. I want
a singleness of eye, a purity of intention, a central
core to my life that will enable me to carry out these
obligations and activities as well as I can. I want, in
fact—to borrow from the language of the saints—to
live "in grace" as much of the time as possible.

—ANNE MORROW LINDBERGH

When all else fails, try gratitude. Sometimes, that's
what we're supposed to be learning. If we can't
think of anything to be grateful about, be grateful
anyway. Will gratitude. Fake it if necessary.

—PIA MELLODY

The season of Lent and the sometimes dreary days of early
March provide a good opportunity for us to remember to
practice gratitude, which nourishes and fortifies our inner peace.

As I mentioned earlier, Brother David Steindl-Rast distin-
guishes between being grateful *in* a situation and grateful *for*
a situation, and I learned about that distinction firsthand in
a "gratitude boot camp" one year when my very healthy husband, Jack, had some serious eye issues.

In late January, a few days after we'd buried my mother-in-
law, Jack discovered he had a detached retina and immediately
went through the uncomfortable procedure to fix it. (Imagine

being fully awake and having a needle stuck into your wide-open eye.) His spirits were good afterward, and we looked forward to continued health for him. But less than two weeks later, another detachment occurred in the same eye. Jack again had it repaired. For ten more weeks, this scenario repeated itself several times. Jack would have the procedure, recover for a few days, think he was out of the woods, and then another detachment would occur. Through it all, Jack, a high school teacher, continued teaching his advanced placement physics classes each morning. He requested that the surgeries be performed in the afternoon, and he would return to school the next day.

By the time he had his fifth operation, the doctor informed him that if it didn't "take," Jack would be facing more invasive surgery and perhaps eventually the loss of vision in his eye. The chance of this happening was devastating to both of us. I reminded myself that even if he lost his vision completely, we could still be grateful for our life together. Sure, it would be diminished in some ways. But he would still be here. I thought of all the women who had lost their partners suddenly, who would be incredibly thankful to have them back, vision or no vision. Focusing on what I still *had* instead of what I might not have allowed me to keep a semblance of positivity, which Jack desperately needed at the time.

Fortunately for us, that fifth surgery was his last and we were able to return to our "normal" life soon afterward. But the experience of almost losing something so integral to our lives made us appreciative of all the gifts we so easily take for granted, day in and day out.

# Putting the Wisdom into Practice

Challenging circumstances can teach us so much. Perhaps you are dealing with a difficult situation right now. Can you think of something to be grateful for *in* the situation? Is there anything good that can or might come from it? As best-selling author Father James Martin explains, "Gratitude is the foundation of the spiritual life."

# Week Three

Only when we are no longer afraid
do we begin to live.
—DOROTHY THOMPSON

The other side of every fear is freedom.
—MARILYN FERGUSON

When I played volleyball in college, our team was flying home from a tournament in Minnesota and we encountered a severe thunderstorm. The little aircraft carrying my eight team members and two coaches hit turbulence, and our plane seemed to be dropping from the sky. The two flight attendants aboard ran screaming to the back of the plane. I clutched my friend's hand beside me and began praying for dear life. The plane continued dropping and dropping, tossing back and forth for what seemed like forever. After many minutes, we finally leveled off and eventually landed without much more trouble. (We clapped exuberantly when the wheels touched down.)

On every subsequent flight I took, I was filled with dread and terror. I watched other passengers calmly reading their newspapers while my heart raced with panic. This anxiousness affected the quality of my life several days before each trip. I would grow nervous, depressed, and agitated. I wouldn't share my fears with people because they sounded ridiculous and irrational, which they were. Finally, after years of misery, I took steps to conquer my fear. Here's some of the advice I followed:

1. Be vulnerable and acknowledge your fear. I could clearly see the damage the fear was doing to me and our family. It's helpful to keep a log to own your fears and track the progress of your efforts to overcome them.

2. Ask yourself how the fear came about: What is its history, what triggers it, how does it affect you? Does this fear control your mind and behavior? My fear of flying began with a frightening event and created significant emotional reactions that were unhealthy.

3. Imagine the outcome you desire. I didn't want to be miserable days ahead of every flight, and I wanted to stop reacting to every bump and tilt of the plane. Whatever outcome you want, keep that goal in mind to motivate your actions.

4. Educate yourself about the realities of your fears. I read about the safety of airline travel, talked to pilots, and listened to others who had overcome their fear of flying. I learned strategies to calm myself during flights, and practiced these every time I boarded a plane. In the beginning, I had to talk to myself like a child, *Time to breathe deeply and calm yourself, Anne.* This kept my mind from racing ahead to the *I'm gonna die* story I'd been telling myself for so long. And stories of frequent fliers who'd dispelled their fears gave me hope that I too could be successful.

After a year or two of work, I finally conquered my fear of flying. What freedom! Now I look forward to my frequent flights, grateful for the time to disconnect, read, and relax. I rarely even remember my old fear, and am forever thankful for that.

## Putting the Wisdom into Practice

Do you have a fear you'd like to overcome? It can be big or small, but if it's one you'd rather not keep lugging around, consider the four steps above. Look your fear in the eye and plan how you'd like to conquer it. Imagine the freedom you'll experience when your fear is put to bed. Now go for it! You won't regret it.

# Week Four

To send a letter is a good way to go somewhere
without moving anything but your heart.

—PHYLLIS THEROUX

This is not a letter, but my arms
around you for a brief moment.

—KATHERINE MANSFIELD

One March day about twenty years ago, I received a hand-addressed envelope in my post office box with a red trolley near the return address, and this note inside:

Dear Ms. Kernion,
What beautiful cards you are making! I bought several "Cards by Anne" and simply wanted to congratulate you and thank you for your obvious care.
    Grace and Peace,
    Fred Rogers

I was so surprised! And excited! Mister Rogers was buying my cards! His simple, thoughtful note in his beautiful handwriting now hangs in our card packaging area, where I see it every day. I later discovered that Mister Rogers regularly sent affirming notes to those who touched him in big and small ways. Just think of how much joy he spread through that practice!

As the owner of and artist for a greeting card company, I am often asked, "Do people still send cards?" "Of course they do!" I reply. In our world of emails and text messages, hand-written letters are cherished even more, no matter who sends them, famous or not-so-famous. Don't we all feel happy when we look into the mailbox and see a hand-addressed envelope instead of the usual stack of bills, catalogs, donation requests, and advertisements? Aren't we glad to know that someone has thought of us, spent time selecting a card, writing a note, and stamping and addressing the envelope? When I receive a note that is particularly meaningful, it gets tucked into a book for later discovery or added to the file folder in my office titled "Letters Worth Saving." Then I can experience the joy and warmth of reading the letter again and again.

We can't reread phone calls. And do you know anyone who has a box of printed-out emails or Twitter messages? I don't. What I *do* have is a box of hundreds of letters Jack and I exchanged while living many miles apart before we became engaged. I imagine us in our rocking chairs thirty years from now, rereading them to each other with tears in our eyes.

Handwritten notes add beauty to our lives in many ways:

- Personal notes can have a profound effect on the recipient. Do you know it usually takes only five to seven "real" letters to persuade an elected official to investigate an issue?
- Thoughtful letters can affirm our connections to others in our families and our communities.

- When we pause and express our thoughts through a handwritten note, we cultivate the art of "gracious living."
- It is so comforting to have something tangible and meaningful to hold on to and reread when life is tossing us about and our souls need the voice of a friend or loved one to buoy us up.

There is something about the process of putting pen to paper, in our own unique handwriting, that draws on a deeper part of our beings and allows us to express emotions that might be difficult to express face-to-face. Plus, because it is a more physical, organic endeavor—and more time-consuming—than typing an email, we take time to choose our words carefully, perhaps conveying sentiments we feel deep within and might not be able to adequately express out loud. Emails may be time-savers but handwritten notes are "time-savors."

## Putting the Wisdom into Practice

Do you know one person who could use a pick-me-up note? Someone who might be struggling with a decision or a difficulty in their lives? Maybe someone who has suffered a loss or is homebound? Take time this week to write a note—or two or three—of encouragement, affirmation, or friendship. It needn't be long, just a few sentences can express a lot. Let others know you are thinking of them. It will brighten their day *and* yours.

# APRIL

# Week One

There is a sun within every person.

—RUMI

Do you know what you are? You are a marvel. In
all the world there is no other exactly like you.

—PABLO CASALS

On a Thursday night in Pittsburgh, I stood in line to board
a flight. I'd like to say I was in a patient mood but, truth-
fully, I was a bit harried and eager to get away for the holiday
weekend. A woman near me was talking quite loudly, and I
had an uncharitable thought or two: *Can't she keep her voice
down? Most of us don't want to be a part of her private conversation.*
When I glanced toward her, I discovered she was an adult with
special needs and I felt the weight of my judgment.

I began listening and observing her and the two young men
flanking her. Immediately I was touched by their patience
and kindness. She instructed the twenty-one-year-old seated

to her right to "Call your girlfriend and tell her you're thinking of her. She would really like that!" He smiled and said he would call her as soon as she returned home; don't worry. Then the woman declared her excitement about going on vacation. "We're going to fly on an airplane!" This exclamation caused everyone around us to smile. A few moments later, the gate agent announced, "We've found a small address book, black with gold trim. If it is yours, please come retrieve it." The woman replied loudly, as though the agent were only speaking to her, "Nope! It's not mine! Mine has flowers. And it's pretty! It's not black. That's not mine!" Again, many of us smiled, appreciating her enthusiasm and innocence.

A few days later, I heard an Irish priest proclaim: "We are all bearers of light, even though none of us is flawless or untarnished. Light shines out of darkness." It was a welcome reminder that each of us carries a spark within us, no matter what faults or limitations we have. He encouraged us to give to the world whatever unique gifts we have, and not to hide them for fear they might not be perfect. I thought of the cheer this special woman had brought to others that night at the airport, and was glad to have witnessed her gift: simple, unaffected joy. She reminded me that our light need not dazzle or blind, but it is light the world needs, and everyone's beam can help dispel darkness.

Here's to the light within every one of us.

## Putting the Wisdom into Practice

Can you recall a time when you made a hasty judgment and then discovered something that caused you to rethink it? This week, take time to notice when your judging mind.jumps to a conclusion that may or may not be charitable or correct. Try replacing the judgment with compassion and kindness. Imagine a good reason why someone might act in the way you judge as "wrong." See how much more warmth and connection you feel toward others.

This practice is also effective when you catch yourself harshly judging yourself. Cultivating self-compassion is something we all need to work on. Think about at least one gift you have, one that others notice and acknowledge. This is how you bring light to the world. Be sure to let that light shine this week. Your light and gifts help dispel the darkness.

# Week Two

It is impossible to live without failing at something, unless you live so cautiously that you might as well not have lived at all.

—J. K. ROWLING

By taking just a few extra seconds to stay with a positive experience—even the comfort in a single breath—you'll help turn a passing mental state into lasting neural structure.

—RICK HANSON

In *Hardwiring Happiness*, psychologist Dr. Rick Hanson explores how we can change our thinking to cultivate happiness, and provides insightful lessons for emotional and spiritual growth. Hanson delineates the root causes of suffering, both biological and psychological, explaining that our brains have been hardwired to respond to negative experiences like Velcro and to positive experiences like Teflon. Thousands of years ago, our ancestors needed to be keenly aware of all the dangers, sometimes life-threatening, that lurked around every rock, bush, and tree. But this vigilance that helped humans survive ten thousand years ago now creates stress and anxiety in us. We hang on to difficult and painful events and often forget the joyous ones soon after they end. We store negative experiences as though our lives depended on them, which may have been true eons ago but is definitely not the case today. Conversely, we experience great joys yet often don't take them in and fully appreciate their beauty. Positive events can slip through our memories, barely making an impression on our brains.

Can you remember a biting comment or nasty email from years ago like I can? Truth be told, I can probably recall the sender's name, where they lived, maybe even their job title. Without much prodding, I can still feel the deep pain and sadness. But how helpful is that skill? And what about all of those wonderful compliments that came my way, day in and day out? Where have those gone?

To thwart this tendency to hold on to the bad and discard the good, Hanson recommends lingering on positive experiences to embed them deeper in our minds. "Savor the good times!" he reminds us. We will then appreciate the blessings that *do* come our way, and when we count them again and again, they will stick in our memories longer. Over time, these small, positive rememberings add up to large changes in our brains. As we search for blessings each and every day, we train our brains to find good even in unexpected places.

# Putting the Wisdom into Practice

This week, be aware of the ways you dwell on difficult or unpleasant incidents. Try to let them go. Be Teflon. Do you recall the last time your heart started pounding when you were in a less-than-life-threatening situation? When that happens, use this technique to help defuse your reaction: Inhale deeply through your nose, drawing breath from even the lower third of your lungs, hold it for a count of four, and then exhale slowly through your mouth or nose, allowing the exhalation to last six or eight counts, if possible. This exercise tamps down your sympathetic nervous system, the fight-or-flight response, and will help you "just be" with any discomfort without reacting further, helping to decrease your anxiety.

# Week Three

Mindfulness ... is the direct opposite
of taking life for granted.

—JON KABAT-ZINN

Be happy in the moment—that's enough.
Each moment is all we need, not more.

—MOTHER TERESA

Paying attention, or being mindful, is a keystone spiritual practice. It is a way to nurture deep states of relaxation, to remember to be grateful and accepting, and to call to mind the presence of God, which all help defuse tension in ourselves and others. Mindfulness also aids in reducing stress and increases our concentration and focus.

Seventeenth-century monk Brother Lawrence used all the mundane moments in his kitchen to simply "practice the presence of God." He would give "a little glance to God," noting that the essence of the spiritual life is "offering God your heart whenever you can."[1]

There are many easy ways to incorporate mindfulness into our daily activities. I try to use a variety of available cues, particularly chores and repetitive tasks that can be invitations to mindfulness, instead of dreading them and wishing the time away to move on to more important things. When I'm watering my plants, I simply bring my attention to the plants. I focus on the leaves, taking note of which ones are brown. I watch the water seep into the soil and rejoice when I see new shoots forming. I try to refrain from thinking about what I'm going to do when the watering is completed. With thirty plants in my house, this takes a while. I treat this time as a meditative break and enjoy the interlude in my day.

Using the practice of mindfulness, we return to the present in a patient, nonjudgmental way. Time doesn't slip away meaninglessly. We are awake in the moment, enjoying the feeling of complete wholeness.

# Putting the Wisdom into Practice

There are several other activities I use to maintain mindfulness. Perhaps try one or more this week.

1. Drink your tea or coffee at half-speed. Stop and really experience the flavor, the warmth of the beverage, the feel of the cup in your hands, and breathe slowly.

2. Slow down at mealtime and really taste your food. How often do we finish a meal and not even remember what we tasted? We often appreciate our meals when we dine out. Bring that awareness to your home-cooked meals.

3. When taking out the trash or walking the dog at night, pause, look up at the sky, and listen to the crickets or the sounds around you.

4. Mindfully wash dishes, feeling the touch of the dish in your hands, noticing the warmth of the water on your skin. Wash each piece more slowly than usual, keeping your

attention on the dishes, the fragrance of the soap, the gift of running water.

5. Make use of waiting time for mindful moments. As you wait in line, at a red light or stop sign, while you're waiting for your computer to boot up in the morning, pause, look around you, breathe deeply, and relax into the moment.

6. Take time to appreciate nature. When walking in the woods, weeding the garden, or cutting the grass, note the smells, the faint sounds, and the breeze.

7. Open and close doors mindfully, bringing yourself back to the moment.

8. When folding laundry, take a deep breath and carefully lift each piece of clothing out of the basket. Gently fold it and place it on its stack.

9. Practice yoga, tai chi, or listening to music to promote mindfulness.

# Week Four

I think that no matter how old or infirm I may become, I will always plant a large garden in the spring. Who can resist the feelings of hope and joy that one gets from participating in nature's rebirth?

—EDWARD GIOBBI

All life holds within itself a promise of resurrection.

—GABRIEL MARCEL

In late March a few years ago, I lost a friend who was ten years younger than me. He seemed to be in excellent physical condition, someone we assumed had decades of life ahead of him. His sudden death shocked and saddened everyone who knew him. Losing someone so young makes all of us realize—again—how important it is to truly live each day and tell our loved ones *today* how much they mean to us.

On the heels of that loss, we then experienced elation: our new grandson was born, arriving a week early to boot! From his very first days, he was a calm, content, healthy baby, and for that we could only rejoice and share the happy news with everyone who would listen. It's truly a wonder how much happiness a new life brings to the world. We visit with him several times a week through the marvels of FaceTime technology, and delight in watching him grow and change every day as he takes in this new world of his. Our hearts are filled to the brim.

At the end of his life, neurologist and best-selling author Oliver Sacks captured a similar and profound sense of gratitude that can guide our quest for a full and meaningful life:

> I feel intensely alive, and I want and hope in the time that remains to deepen my friendships, to say farewell to those I love.... I feel a sudden clear focus and perspective. There is no time for anything inessential.
>
> My predominant feeling is one of gratitude. I have loved and been loved; I have been given much and I have given something in return. Above all, I have been a sentient being on this beautiful planet, and that in itself has been an enormous privilege and adventure.

Wherever this April day finds you, remember to embrace each moment, keeping your eyes open like a newborn baby, scanning the world for common delights and everyday beauty. That is a lesson we can find in life and death and resurrection.

# Putting the Wisdom into Practice

Read again the words of Oliver Sacks. We can take some wisdom from him, someone living his last days on earth, and apply it to our lives this week. Remember that each day is a gift, one that we ought not take for granted. What would you do differently today if you knew you weren't going to be here next week? Be softer and kinder with everyone you meet.

# MAY

## Week One

Here is your life. You might never have
been, but you are because the party wouldn't
have been complete without you.

—FREDERICK BUECHNER

Life is an improvisational art at every age.

—MARY CATHERINE BATESON

A few years ago, our son, Jackson, mentioned a book he
thought I'd find interesting: *The Top Five Regrets of the
Dying*. In it, author Bronnie Ware, a hospice nurse, shares what
her patients voice most frequently in their last days:

1. "I wish I'd had the courage to live a life true to myself,
   not the life others expected of me." This was the most
   common regret of all. Lesson: Think about what matters most to you, what your deepest values are, and

what you hope for in life. Begin living with those ideals in mind before it's too late.

2. "I wish I hadn't worked so hard." Lesson: Examine your job commitments and daily choices to see if there is a way to fashion a life that requires less money. The "tiny house" movement is one version of how few material goods some of us need to have a happy life. Many of these homeowners express great joy at the freedom they now have as a result of living with less "stuff."

3. "I wish I'd had the courage to express my feelings." Many patients regretted conforming to what others expected of them to be instead of risking "rocking the boat." Some carried resentment and bitterness for decades, causing health problems. Lesson: We take a chance by being honest, but it will create healthier relationships in the long run.

4. "I wish I'd stayed in touch with my friends." Lesson: Old friends are treasures. Don't let yourself get busy with life and fail to make the effort to stay in touch with them.

5. "I wish I'd let myself be happier." Lesson: Do yourself a favor and allow yourself to be happy. You only have this one life, and being discontented doesn't help anyone, least of all yourself. Why waste even one day deciding to be miserable? It *is* a decision. Choose happiness.[1]

# Putting the Wisdom into Practice

Spend a few moments each day this week pondering the five regrets.

1. Do you have any dreams that you still haven't pursued? What is stopping you? Being "too old" and believing "it's too late" are not excuses. Remember Grandma Moses began painting when she was seventy-eight years young. Take the world into your arms! Take a few baby steps toward that dream this week.

2. Are you spending some time each day "smelling the roses"? If not, figure out a way to bring some enjoyment to every day. None of us wants to end up, as poet Mary Oliver warns, having simply "visited this world."

3. When or with whom do you find yourself being not completely honest? How might you change that? You'll be much healthier and happier if you choose honesty.

4. Is there an old friend or two you think about but haven't communicated with recently? Write a note, send an email, or just pick up the phone and call. It'll bring joy to both of you. Who doesn't want to reconnect with former friends and reminisce about old times?

5. Can you find something to rejoice in every day, even if you are facing significant challenges right now? As Abraham Lincoln said, "Most people are about as happy as they make up their minds to be."

# Week Two

Clearing out clutter opens us up
to the wonders that await.

—KATRINA MAYER

Don't own so much clutter that you will be
relieved to see your house catch fire.

—WENDELL BERRY

I t is a real puzzle to me why springtime—and *only* springtime—
ignites a desire in me to clean and de-clutter my house.
Perhaps shedding layers of winter clothing reminds me of the
need to shed some possessions, too. When I'm able to rid our
house of the unnecessary to allow for more visual and mental space, I'm more relaxed, creative, and effective. Inevitably,
though, I lose steam or get sidetracked and never completely
finish the job.

Last year, my daughter Elizabeth recommended *The Life-
Changing Magic of Tidying Up* by Marie Kondo, which is filled
with great tips. Her primary directive is this: When de-cluttering,
take each item in your hands and ask, *Does this spark joy?* If
it does, keep it. If not, discard it. She admonishes us to keep
things that speak to our hearts and then donate or pitch the
rest. It's that simple and that difficult. So I've begun to ask that
question of many household items, and I find it's a good yard-
stick that allows me to relinquish more items than usual.

Kondo explains there are two reasons why we can't let go of something: either we are attached to the past or we are fearful of the future. If the article brings back a fond memory, we find it hard to toss aside. If that's the case for me, I take a picture of it. But what if we need an item at some future date? Chances are, we really won't. If we do, there are alternate ways to get what we need. Kondo explains that if we acknowledge these two obstacles, attachment and fear, we can overcome their hold on us.

There is something about an uncluttered space that frees our minds, lifts our spirits, and gives us the sense of being "unburdened." It's also gratifying to imagine others using our possessions, because the items we don't need can serve other people. That alone can bring us great pleasure.

Ultimately, Kondo wants to share the benefits of a tidy home: contentment with the things we own and less desire for "more." We can then bask in a sense of peace and pour ourselves into what brings us the most joy: our mission in life.

She has motivated me to move from cupboard to cupboard, room to room, looking at each possession and deciding whether it brings me joy. I'm working in the sequence Kondo recommends: clothing first, then books (oh no!), papers, miscellany, and, lastly, mementos. It may take some time to finish, but I'm looking forward to the wonders that await when the clutter is gone!

## Putting the Wisdom into Practice

What Marie Kondo is advising us to do is what might be called mindful de-cluttering. Start with one cupboard and hold each item. Ask yourself whether it brings you joy. If not, give it away or throw it away. Finish the cupboard and do another on day two. Maybe try a closet or go through your clothes. I guarantee you will feel lighter, freer, more alive after a few cupboards or closets are tidied. Keep going from one room to another. Remember that by saying good-bye to used or unwanted items, you are gifting them to people who need and can use your possessions. And without so many things to keep track of, you'll have more energy to do the things that are *really* important—those activities that bring joy to you and others.

# Week Three

Many people, as they become spiritual, seek "selfless service" in order to deepen their compassion for others. But if you want selfless service, all you need do is have children.

—STEPHEN AND ONDREA LEVINE

Everybody knows how to raise children, except the people who have them.

—P. J. O'ROURKE

As we celebrate Mother's Day this month, I think of my own mom and how I didn't fully appreciate her efforts until I had children. Mom took our education very seriously. My siblings and I attended good Catholic schools. Music lessons were mandatory, and learning two instruments was better than one. Our house was filled with books, encyclopedias, and instructive games. Family vacations were planned around visiting historically important sites. Our trip to the Florida beach included a side excursion to Cape Canaveral and to St. Augustine. A drive to Colorado was the perfect opportunity to visit the birthplace of President Dwight D. Eisenhower. We may have groaned a bit at the time, but now I appreciate that my parents took the time and energy to cart us around to music lessons and educational venues.

But the most important lessons my mom taught us revolved around how we should live. For example, we weren't allowed to buy Mattel products—ever—because Mom didn't approve of Barbie. How could she let her daughters play with a doll whose sole goal in life was to land a date with Ken? She also often reminded us, "All of us put on our pants one leg at a time. Treat everyone with respect and care, no matter who they are." (Except the toy makers at Mattel, I guess!) She firmly believed in the dignity of each person, and didn't want us to ever think we were better, or worse, than anyone else.

I recently found a list of "things we should say every day," compiling advice our mothers might give us:

1. "Thank you. That was great how you …" Praise and thank someone. It doesn't cost anything and will make a big difference to the recipient. Let them know how much you appreciate their efforts. Don't aim for a lengthy speech; just make a small comment indicating you noticed their good deed or competent actions.

2. "I'm sorry I didn't …" We're human. We all make mistakes. So just fess up and say you're sorry for what you did, what you said, or what you didn't do but should have. It will right a wrong and perhaps heal a relationship. Plan what you're going to say, say it, take the blame, and let it go. This gets easier with practice.

3. "Can you help me …?" Isn't it great when someone values your skills in a particular area? We're happy to be recognized for what we do well. If you're asking

someone for help, usually that person will be delighted you value them.

4. "Can I help you …?" When asking this, be specific so the recipient knows where you think you can help. For example: "I have extra tables and chairs. Can I bring them to your party?" or "Do you need a ride to the meeting?" or "Let me carry that bag of groceries to your car."

5. "I love you." It's never a bad time to tell others we love and care about them. Say it frequently and abundantly. Expressing your feelings costs nothing, but is priceless to the people with whom you share them.

# Putting the Wisdom into Practice

1. Recall the ways your own mother taught you how to live. If you can, thank her for all of her efforts. Be specific. She will love hearing a story or two about her younger years. Remember the advice from happiness scholars—savor the good.

2. Look at the list of things we should say every day and choose one or two. Say them to friends, family, co-workers, or neighbors. You'll be glad you did.

# Week Four

Nothing is worth more than this day.
> —JOHANN WOLFGANG VON GOETHE

If I had my life to live over, I would start barefoot
earlier in the spring and stay that way later in the fall.
> —NADINE STAIR

We have many special days that honor particular people,
such as Mother's Day and Father's Day. Thich Nhat
Hanh, the Vietnamese Buddhist monk, suggests that we also
have a "Today's Day" celebration. This day would need no formal announcement, special gifts, or fancy dinners. On this day,
we would not worry about tomorrow or think about yesterday.
We would just live happily in the present moment, enjoying
the gifts of this day. Yes, the past month or week may have
been splendid—or maybe not. Yes, we may have much to look
forward to in the future. But tomorrow has not yet come, and
yesterday is gone. All we really have is today, the most important day of our lives.

A 2010 Harvard study found that people spend 47 percent
of their days thinking about things other than what they're
actually doing. That means half the time we aren't even "there"
to enjoy the present moment. We are somewhere in the past,
perhaps regretting something we said or did. Or maybe we
are worrying about the future, about what might or might

not happen, wasting our precious time on something we have little or no control over. Is this really how we want to spend our valuable time? Not even being present to our lives as they unfold? What happenings are we missing by being so distracted? Who are we not fully listening to? What beauty—and there certainly is beauty—are we missing because our minds are somewhere else?

Hanh suggests that we breathe in and breathe out, remembering that today is the day that we can look at other people with kindness, smile, and be happy that we have the gift of life. Today is the day to live.

# Putting the Wisdom into Practice

Every day this week, as the first thing you do each day, maybe even before you get out of bed, breathe in and breathe out several times. Remind yourself that *today* you are grateful for the gift of life. *Today* is a day you can be particularly kind. *Today* is a day when you can drop the worry, the regret, the fretting. *Today* is the day you will stay in the moment and take in the simple joys it can offer to you. *Today* you can look at other people and smile. When you begin worrying about tomorrow or what happened yesterday, come back to *this* day, this very moment, remembering to live in the present. For *this* moment, right now, is the most important moment you have.

# JUNE

## Week One

Wherever you go, go with all your heart.

—CONFUCIUS

The only ones who will be truly happy are
those who will find a way to serve.

—ALBERT SCHWEITZER

Graduation season is in full swing in early June, as we
launch young adults into the world with pomp and cir-
cumstance, exhorting them to serve others with their gifts and
skills. The part I like best is the commencement address. I love
listening to what an accomplished adult thinks young people
should hear at such a critical juncture in their lives.

Mister Rogers reminded graduates at Marquette University:

> Nobody else can live the life you live. And even though
> no human being is perfect, we always have the chance
> to bring what's unique about us to life in a redeeming

way. It's a miracle when we finally discover whom we're best equipped to serve, when we can best appreciate the unique life we've been given.[1]

Author and journalist Pamela Druckerman told recent graduates to "find their place" in the world, "pay attention to what you're doing on the side," and fill "down" time with things that feed their work and their souls. This might be the inspiration for work you've never considered. As an engineering student, I'd use study breaks to get out my colorful markers, select sayings from my collection of quote books, decorate the top of blank pieces of paper, and write letters to my friends. My roommate Jill, who is now a physician, laughs that my little hobby became my life's work. If only I'd known then what I know now. Think of all the calculus problems I could have skipped!

Novelist David Foster Wallace reminds us that "the real value of education has almost nothing to do with knowledge, and everything to do with simple awareness; awareness of what is so real and essential, so hidden in plain sight all around us." He goes on to say that truly caring about other people and sacrificing for them over and over in myriad ways every day is what real freedom and being educated are all about. Amen to that.

Lastly, George Saunders, an English professor at Syracuse University, gave his audience of graduates just one piece of advice: Be kind. If there was one thing he regretted in his life, it was not being kind to those who needed it. We don't know what burdens others are carrying, so be kind, *especially* to those who aren't exuding warm fuzzies. They probably need it most.

If I were invited to give a commencement address, my message would be this:

> Don't look to the world to tell you what to do. Look deep within yourself and be the unique person you were made to be. No one said it better than Howard Thurman: "Ask yourself what makes you come alive and do that. Because what the world needs is people who have come alive."
>
> No matter what lies ahead, we can all take the counsel of Confucius: "Go with all your heart." To those "going" somewhere in the next few weeks—to a new job, a new school, a new home, a new stage of life—as well as those staying where they are, that advice is spot on. Throw yourselves into the next phase or season, try something new, and say yes to life.

## Putting the Wisdom into Practice

No matter what your age, it's good to ask yourself: *Am I being kind to those I encounter each day, even (especially) those I might view as less fortunate, less educated, or less productive? Is there something new I've thought about trying but haven't?* (If so, give it a go!) *How am I treating those I love? Am I living with "all my heart"?* Take some time this week to think about the messages contained in these speeches and see whether one or more speaks particularly to you.

# Week Two

Only when we tarry do we touch the holy.

—RAINER MARIA RILKE

Let us have fantasy, boldness, unexpectedness, enchantment—above all, tenderness.

—GEORGES BIZET

O ur family recently marked the beginning of summer with a wedding in San Francisco, where our son married his college sweetheart. We enjoyed a few days of activities, including a fun-filled rehearsal picnic featuring a water balloon contest, sack races, and a beanbag toss. We also celebrated what it means to be "Real" à la *The Velveteen Rabbit*. Our daughters chose this excerpt to read during the wedding ceremony:

> Real isn't how you are made," said the Skin Horse....
> "It's a thing that happens to you. You become. It takes a
> long time.... Generally, by the time you are Real, most
> of your hair has been loved off, and your eyes drop
> out and you get loose in the joints and very shabby.
> But these things don't matter at all, because once you
> are Real you can't be ugly, except to people who don't
> understand."[2]

To Jackson's surprise, we brought his childhood companion, a well-worn stuffed animal ingeniously named "Bear" to the reception, reminding all of us of the unfiltered, unconditional love that children exude. During my toast, I held Bear and recounted how tenderly Jackson loved and cared for him throughout his early life. We knew back then that Jackson would make a kind and considerate partner if he simply expressed his affection for another person as he did for his beloved Bear. Then we formally bequeathed Bear to Antonia and Jackson, reminding them to be Real and softhearted with each other. When the toasts ended, Antonia took Bear in her arms, cradling him as she walked from table to table, showing guests his threadbare belly and numerous stitches.

The advice from the Skin Horse is also apropos for the rest of us. As a popular inspirational saying goes, "Love like you've never been hurt." Is it possible to allow others to see our hearts, to feel our compassion and love? To cry without embarrassment when we are deeply moved? If so, we will become Real, fully alive and truly beautiful. We will be able to love and be loved fully, without shields of armor blocking the way.

My hope is that we can begin these summer months by softening our hearts, caring for others, and perhaps tasting a bit of "heaven on earth" along the way.

# Putting the Wisdom into Practice

In what ways do you protect yourself and put up a shield? Do you hold back your impulse to be moved by suffering or pain in others? Perhaps try to soften in the midst of pain—yours or others'—and move toward the discomfort. Open your heart and allow the real you to show, with cracks and blemishes, letting go of the need to look shiny and new.

# Week Three

Our identity is to be found not in
what we do, but in who we are.

—THOMAS MERTON

To be creative means to be in love with life.
You can be creative only if you love life enough
that you want to enhance its beauty, you want
to bring a little more music to it, a little more
poetry to it, a little more dance to it.

—OSHO

Each of us has creative potential, and we use our creative
talents in many ways in our work and home lives, and in
our hobbies. Just think of the meals you create, the gatherings
you host, the meetings you attend. Creativity is needed for all
of those and more. We all can benefit from a boost in our creative juices.

Nothing derails creativity like constant busyness, as research
clearly shows. Studies also tell us that unusual and beautiful
surroundings help us see situations from multiple viewpoints,
illuminating unique solutions to problems. Walking in those
surroundings seems to be better for our brains than just sitting and taking in the scenery. When we focus attention on the
view as we walk or run on a trail, part of our brain is left free
to make associations we might not normally make and produce

original solutions and outcomes. So that old adage to "take a walk to clear your head" has been proven true.

Here are other suggestions that can help spur our creativity:

1. Don't overfocus on the end result, which can cause anxiety. Break the task into steps and work on them one at a time.

2. Plan breaks. Step away from your work and come back to it later to improve your focus.

3. Higher ceilings, such as those found in churches and atriums, encourage abstract thinking. Find an area with an abundance of overhead space and sit. (Works for me every time!)

4. Daydream, reflect, or nap. But do some work first before taking that snooze. If thinking hasn't begun in earnest, the nap won't produce new ideas and solutions.

5. Exercise. Regular cardiovascular exercise helps increase blood and brain serotonin levels. Serotonin puts us in a good mood and helps promote creativity. Take a brisk walk before or during brainstorming meetings. Subconscious creative processes are aided by any exercise that gets your heart pumping. (This is my go-to method for spurring creativity.)

6. Really *look* at art or attentively *listen* to music. Be particularly observant of everything, everywhere—textures, colors, shadings, layouts, framing, placement, the feel of things.

7. Go into nature. Listen to grasshoppers, the wind, rustling leaves, raindrops. An added bonus is that sunlight increases serotonin levels.

8. Diversifying your experiences helps you break your cognitive patterns, leading you to think more flexibly and creatively. Travel to a new destination. Take part in a new, different activity, like ziplining, sailing, a cooking class, bird-watching, or attending a concert that exposes you to new music.

9. Make sure your group has diversity, too. New perspectives, talents, and backgrounds will challenge your thinking and push everyone's creativity beyond its typical boundaries. The business world has recognized that having more diverse corporate boards, and specifically having more women on them, benefits the businesses and the overall economy.[3]

10. Strong emotions like love can drive creativity. Watch inspiring videos and movies, or read an uplifting story.

11. Surround yourself with positive people. Nothing kills creativity more than negativity.

12. Aim to get more sleep and reduce stress in your life. Lack of sleep has a negative effect on our brain's response to serotonin. And stress causes our cortisol levels to rise, which blocks the effect of serotonin.

13. Eat a high-protein breakfast and work on your most important task first thing each day, when serotonin

levels are highest. Proteins in our bodies are converted into serotonin and dopamine, neurotransmitters that are needed to keep our creativity humming along.

14. Shape your workspace. Fill it with meaningful objects (I have small stacks of stones in every room, souvenirs from vacations) and eliminate clutter if it distracts you.

## Putting the Wisdom into Practice

Creativity is a pathway to happiness. Are there creative avenues you'd like to explore? Set aside time to experiment this week, even for thirty minutes. Choose one or two suggestions from the list above when you have a problem to solve.

# Week Four

The Journey is essential to the dream.

—FRANCIS OF ASSISI

We must let go of the life we have planned, so
as to accept the one that is waiting for us.

—JOSEPH CAMPBELL

After working the busiest conference of the year in the
Los Angeles area, I was looking forward to spending a
few days at a monastery in the Rocky Mountains. Anxious to
finally get there and just "be" for a few days, I departed from
Denver's airport around 10 a.m. for a drive that was estimated
to take three and a half hours. About an hour into the trip,
traffic slowed to a standstill due to an accident. After forty-five
minutes of sitting, all of us were escorted off the road and onto
a detour that took us through some small towns surrounded
by beautiful scenery. I told myself that this detour was no big
deal and that the views were compensating for the delay, which
they were. So far, so good.

Back on Interstate 70 and finally going the speed limit, I continued to enjoy the spectacular mountains in front of me and
the streams beside the road. Funny thing about those roads:
there are occasional signs calling out, "Scenic view ahead."
*Ahead?* I thought to myself. How about *everywhere*? I laughed

out loud every time I passed one of those signs, thinking, *all* of this, in every direction, is a scenic view!

So I continued on, enjoying the beautiful vistas as I drove. But this good fortune was fleeting. Another accident, this time quite serious, closed the road for several hours. A courteous highway employee advised me to head back to one of the nearby towns and relax for a few hours. "This is going to take a while," he said. Ugh! This trip was *not* going as planned.

The women at the pharmacy in the town of Eagle could not have been more helpful, even offering me yogurt from their lunches to tide me over. They guided me to a local eatery, where I settled in with a cup of tea and a good book. Three hours later another stranded traveler received word that the highway was open and I returned to my journey.

So almost nine hours from when I began the drive, I finally arrived at the monastery as the sun was fading over the horizon. I was grateful for the safe trip, particularly after seeing the damage and debris from a serious car accident. (Why does it sometimes take witnessing another's tragedy to get us to count our blessings?) But I was also thankful for the chance encounters with those kind Colorado folks. Sure, there was disappointment that I had lost precious hours of time at the monastery, but I thought about the gems of wisdom I had found on this little trip: I may have a destination, but often when I am only focused on getting there, I miss the little blessings along the way. On top of that, the scenic view can many times be found in the unmarked, ordinary landscapes of our lives.

Sometimes—many times—we learn more on life's detours than we do when all goes according to plan.

# Putting the Wisdom into Practice

We all have disruptions in our well-laid plans. This week, be mindful of those moments when things aren't going quite right, when you are delayed inconveniently, something breaks down, or your goals aren't completed in the time frame you hoped they would be. Take a deep breath and think about the gifts that *are* present in those moments. Ask yourself if you will even remember the inconvenience in a few weeks or months. Try keeping your attention on the wonders of the life you *do* have, not the life you *wish* you had.

# JULY

## Week One

I've never made one of my discoveries
through the process of rational thinking.

—ALBERT EINSTEIN

All shall be well, and all shall be well, and
all manner of things shall be well.

—JULIAN OF NORWICH

Yoga has many proven benefits, and one that has been helpful to me is learning to breathe while holding an uncomfortable, challenging pose. You learn to marshal your concentration and let go of defeating negative thoughts, such as *This is too hard ... I want to give up ... I'm not very good at this ... How much longer can I hold still?* Instead, you focus on just breathing in and breathing out, trying to remain relaxed and balanced, staying with the discomfort.

This lesson has been valuable in so many ways. When life throws us difficult or demanding situations, our motto can be:

"Breathe in. Breathe out. Be calm and steady. Don't run from what is hard." We are not promised a smooth road during our years on earth. Without the rude driver, the inconsiderate office mate, or the obnoxious relative, where would we learn to exercise patience and tolerance, or discover, as my mom would say, our intestinal fortitude? Sometimes the difficult situation is not caused by others but is simply one of life's curveballs, such as a health issue, an accident, or a family crisis.

Staying with tough situations or people is not a simple thing to do. I'd much rather sneak away, ignore the problem or person, or forget anything ever happened. Yet I know this is not a healthy way to deal with tense circumstances. It's also avoiding the opportunity to practice being kind and loving to those who challenge us.

I've found that the discipline of quiet prayer or meditation is extremely helpful. When we sit quietly, just breathing, we learn to hold a space and let our thoughts go for a few minutes. We then create a buffer between the world around us and our reaction to it, and we are able to choose more thoughtful, loving responses to uncomfortable people and situations. Or perhaps we may choose to just stay quiet and *not* respond. The goal is to bring that space, that buffer, into our daily circumstances and know that we have a choice in how we react.

In *The Places That Scare You,* beloved Buddhist teacher Pema Chödrön invites and encourages us to stay with our unpleasant feelings. As a species, we seem to have a low tolerance for uneasiness. But if we can learn to stay with our vulnerabilities, which is what discomfort is all about, to stay with the awkwardness and the anxiousness, then we can cultivate greater levels of patience, understanding, and kindness.

## Putting the Wisdom into Practice

Life usually offers plenty of opportunities to practice staying in difficult situations. This week, bring your awareness to any awkward or tense moments that come up in your day. Watch your reaction. Try to identify what prompts that response, and instead of physically or mentally running away from the tension, try to stay in the moment and bring some compassion to it. See how that pivot in your reaction changes things. Remember, this is a skill most of us need to practice again and again, probably our whole lives.

# Week Two

The purpose of life is to live it, to taste experience to the utmost, to reach out eagerly and without fear for newer and richer experience.

—ELEANOR ROOSEVELT

You know it's summer in Ireland
when the rain gets warmer.

—HAL ROACH

My Irish grandmother was a hoot, even though her life was not an easy one. A beer-drinking nurse, she was widowed in her forties and raised six children on her own. She worked in a hospital full time until the age of seventy-six. Typical of women of her generation, Grandma pinched pennies by making almost everything from scratch, wearing the same simple clothing for years, reusing every jar and tin can, darning holes in socks and gloves, and more. She had little money but a lot of heart and spunk, and I loved her dearly. Grandma was determined, resourceful, and deeply spiritual. But she also knew how to have fun.

One of my favorite memories is attending Game 1 of the 1968 World Series with her in St. Louis. We were seated in the outfield stands. Bob Gibson was on the mound and Curt Flood, my favorite player, was in center field. For a rabid ten-year-old baseball fan, it was a dream come true. But sometime in the early innings, as we were cheering on our beloved Cardinals, Grandma heard one of the men to her right—we were the only females in our section—complaining loudly about "that little girl taking someone's seat." Grandma, beer in hand, leaned over and said to the man, "Sir, I don't think you know what you're talking about. C'mon, Anne, show him what a fan you are!" I began rattling off the averages for Curt Flood, Tim McCarver, Orlando Cepeda, Lou Brock, Dal Maxvill, and more until the man had heard enough and returned to watching the game. Grandma gave me a big grin, indicating we'd won that argument. After the game, elated by our beloved Cardinals' victory, we arrived home and recounted the story to my parents, taking delight in the win, of course, but also in "showing that man a thing or two about who deserves to be at a World Series game!" Lesson #1: Stand up for yourself.

Luckily, I got to spend a lot of time with Grandma Gessner, since she would often babysit my siblings and me. When she did, she'd bring junk food—corn puffs and cheese popcorn that our parents wouldn't buy for us—to eat while we watched forbidden scary movies underneath the covers of our homemade tents. We'd stay up well past our bedtime and race to our rooms when we heard the garage door announcing our parents' arrival. (We'd pretend to be asleep when they checked in on us.) Grandma instructed me on how to make homemade jam from crabapples picked from a neighbor's tree, how to make the best fudge and peanut brittle I've ever tasted, how to properly iron a pillowcase, and how to flip baseball cards. She shared with me the proper technique and exquisite joy of climbing trees, and also how to wordlessly savor the view of a setting sun, one of my last memories of her.

The most important lesson I learned from Grandma, a typically Irish one, was to live each day with good humor, no matter what life might throw at you.

## Putting the Wisdom into Practice

Think of some of your older relatives and the lives they led. What attributes did they pass along to you? What did their lives teach you that might still inspire you? If you are now a grandparent or great-aunt or -uncle, what lessons do you hope to impart to your grandchildren, nieces, and nephews? Jot down some of your thoughts and share them in a note of love and affection.

# Week Three

To find joy in another's joy, that is
the secret of happiness.

—GEORGE BERNANOS

These things I have spoken to you, that my joy
may be in you, and that your joy may be full.

—JOHN 15:11

My extended family celebrated an unexpected and joyous event one recent summer. One of my younger brothers, John, age forty-seven, married Allison, also forty-seven. Neither one had been married before. To say the families were happy for them is quite an understatement. A year earlier, John had visited us to run the Pittsburgh Marathon and confided in Jack and me that he'd given up on finding the right woman. We felt sad for him, knowing how much joy and richness our marriage had brought to our lives.

A few months after John's visit, we traveled to St. Louis to visit my family and spend some time with John again. He couldn't talk enough about this woman he'd recently met, how much he enjoyed spending time with her, and how much he appreciated their long conversations. We held our breath and crossed our fingers, hoping things would work out for him this time.

Allison had adopted a little girl from birth a few years prior to meeting John, and Sadie became John's little friend from the get-go. A few months after her mom and John started dating, the three of them were driving in the car, and Sadie, riding in the backseat, asked her mom, "Mom, could John be my boyfriend, too?" Several months later, Sadie was lying on the couch on a Sunday afternoon, sick with a bad cold. She had gotten wind of the news that her mom and John were buying a house and asked John, "Does this mean we're all going to live together?" John said yes. Then Sadie sidled up to John, put her head on his shoulder, and asked, "Does this mean that you're going to be my daddy?" John asked, "Do you want me to be your daddy?" "Yes! I do!" Sadie replied. John said he could barely keep the tears from running down his face. Sadie looked forward to her first Father's Day with a dad, and was so excited to jump out of bed that Sunday morning, very early, to present John with his first Father's Day gift.

So at the ripe age of forty-seven, my brother has a new family with a little girl who adores him. At the wedding picnic to celebrate their union, John couldn't wipe the smile off his face, and neither could we. As author George Sand remarked, "The greatest happiness in life is to love and be loved."

# Putting the Wisdom into Practice

What can you find to rejoice in this week? Keep your eyes peeled for reasons to take delight in another's good fortune. Send a card or call a friend who's recently received good news. We often take pride in our ability to encourage others when times are hard, but recall that one of the keystone practices of happiness is being happy for others when they have good news to share. Spread some of that happiness around! As the saying goes, shared joy is double joy.

# Week Four

You better cut the pizza in four pieces because
I'm not hungry enough to eat six.

—YOGI BERRA

Life is better than death, I believe, if only because it
is less boring, and because it has fresh peaches in it.

—ALICE WALKER

We receive a box of produce each week from a local farmer. It's always a surprise to find what's inside. Sometimes the veggies are completely unknown to me. Until a few years ago, I had no idea what fennel, turnips, rhubarb, kale, or Swiss chard looked like. Now I actually know how to cook a few of them, to the complete surprise of my family. Cooking isn't one of my strong suits, to say the least!

Lately, the very best items in the boxes have been peaches— the kind that are so juicy that you are sure you've never tasted anything this perfect in your life. When I eat one of these miracles of nature I have to stop everything I'm doing and relish each and every bite, as the juice runs down my chin. A taste like this is so overwhelming, so sweet, so heavenly, that there is no room in my awareness for any other sensation. I am completely present in the act of eating the peach.

Our sense of taste, and other senses as well, can be gateways into the practice of being aware of the gift of life. As Thich

Nhat Hanh explains, eating is "a chance to return to the present moment and stop the rushing and the planning." Eating these local peaches can't help but bring me into awareness by their incredible burst of flavor. They remind me to savor life, to savor the long summer days, and to savor simple pleasures.

One of the reasons we are drawn to travel to new places is that we try new foods and see new sights. We are able to experience these new events more fully because we are more present to them. Our everyday stresses and concerns are back at home, and we often live more in the moment when we are on vacation. No wonder we enjoy ourselves so much when we go away! But it's possible to bring that state of mind home with us, starting with our next meal.

# Putting the Wisdom into Practice

These warmer months in the northern hemisphere offer us innumerable opportunities to practice savoring local produce, colorful flowers, singing birds, walks in nature. This week, practice savoring your food. Perhaps head to a local farm or farmers' market and pick out some produce you've never tried. For the next seven days, try not to eat while doing another activity like walking, driving, or talking. Actually take the time to sit while you eat this week.

At every meal, practice tasting and relishing the different flavors on your plate. Notice the colors, textures, smells, and shapes of your food. Slow down and *experience* each bite, as though it were the first time you ever tasted that particular cuisine. Linger over your meals, taking a few extra moments to be aware of the subtle flavorings. Take a few deep breaths after every few bites. If you're sharing a meal, ask the other person what he or she tastes, what flavors appeal most. After a week of practice, you may find that mealtimes have become oases of calm and stillness, little mini-retreats in your busy days.

# AUGUST

## Week One

What do I really want to do? Long hours of quiet in the woods, reading a little, meditating a lot, walking up and down in the pine needles in bare feet. I can imagine no other joy on earth than to have such a place and be at peace in it, to live in silence, to think and write, to listen to the wind and to all the voices of the woods.

—THOMAS MERTON

Leisure is the balance between work and rest. It is the opposite of idleness because it is the basis from which good work starts and grows.

—BROTHER DAVID STEINDL-RAST

Summer vacations are opportunities to retreat from everyday life and then return with a fresh pair of eyes, observing the everyday and commonplace with renewed gratitude and perspective. But even a simple break of a few hours gives us space to step back and view life with new eyes. I occasionally spend a Saturday afternoon reading in a hammock beneath our maple tree, which proves to be perfectly refreshing for both body and spirit. We are better for everyone when we take time to reassess, read, reflect, walk barefoot, listen to the wind … time to see the world as if for the first time. What wonders are at our feet and fingertips that too often go unnoticed?

I also find I'm most creative and alive if I've managed to strike a healthy balance between work and rest. Dr. Stuart Brown, founder of the National Institute for Play, notes that "play energizes and enlivens us. It eases our burdens, renews our natural sense of optimism, and opens us up to new possibilities."

On a summer day last year, Jack was completing the chore of cutting the grass and trimming the hedges. I happened to be at the kitchen window and stopped for a few moments just to watch him. A burst of gratitude came over me and filled my heart: how fortunate we have been that our trials have been relatively minor, our health good, our children raised. Sure, there have been little and not-so-little hiccups along the way, but all in all, we have shared a good life.

If we don't make time to step back and take in the little moments like this in our lives, we wind up missing all that's truly important. I need to keep reminding myself to stop. Just stop for a moment or two and notice the good all around me. Our life is not perfect. Whose is? But certainly we all have something to appreciate.

# Putting the Wisdom into Practice

Sit in your backyard or a nearby park, noticing the wildflowers, the birds and their sounds, the trees, the water, small creatures—all that is around you. Or engage in a game or activity you enjoy: tennis, charades, a card or board game, perhaps even drawing with crayons or coloring in one of the wonderful adult coloring books available these days—anything that brings some lightness and spontaneity to your day.

# Week Two

In times of stress, the best thing we can do for each other is to listen with our ears and our hearts and to be assured that our questions are just as important as our answers.

—FRED ROGERS

Whatever may be the tensions and the stresses of a particular day, there is always lurking close at hand the trailing beauty of forgotten joy or unremembered peace.

—HOWARD THURMAN

Harvard psychologist Ellen Langer was one of the first researchers of mindfulness, although she has a slightly different take on the subject than most. Langer defines mindfulness as actively "seeking out, creating, and noticing the new." Her research shows that scanning for novelty around us every day will improve our health and competence, and increase our happiness and life span. If we had a pill that could provide all those life-changing benefits, we'd all be taking it!

Langer recommends replacing the ubiquitous phrase "being present" with the term "notice." For example, take time to notice five new things about your friend or spouse. When you do that, the person can't help but respond to you differently.

Langer notes that the consequences of living mindlessly are enormous, causing many physical problems: stress, depression, high blood pressure, sleep disruptions, and GI issues, among other maladies. The quality of our lives is profoundly affected by whether we take notice of our surroundings or not. Langer says that if we bring attention to our immediate environment, we become engaged and enlivened. I love what theologian Marcus Borg says about the wonder of simply being here: "An open heart is alive to wonder, to the sheer marvel of 'isness.' It is remarkable that the world is, that we are here, that we can experience it. The world is not ordinary. Indeed what is remarkable is that it could ever look ordinary to us."[1]

Another area Langer has studied is how we perceive time and negative events. Her motto is, "I'm not going to give up today worrying about tomorrow." Almost all of our worrying is about the future, and we cannot predict what it will bring. Langer recommends asking ourselves, *What am I so worried about?* and *Are there positive things that could happen if I don't finish this task?* Very rarely does our life depend on any one particular action, but we treat what is happening at the moment as the last opportunity we are ever going to have to do that particular thing.

Lastly, Langer cautions us to be careful not to throw all of our emotional energy at a painful event that's taken place. Most difficult episodes are inconveniences, not tragedies. If we become exceedingly upset, we double the negativity and needlessly give the difficulty a piece of our soul, too. It's good to become more aware of our reactions to bad news and try not to make a situation worse than it already is.

# Putting the Wisdom into Practice

What wonders are you missing for lack of awareness? This week, as you go about your daily routines, seek out and notice something new each day. When you drive to the store or to work—keeping your attention on the road, of course!—look around. What details on the route have you overlooked in the past? Scan the faces of your loved ones and friends. Really look into their eyes and take in their unique facial features. What have you missed seeing after all these years? And finally, observe how you react to difficult news this week. Try not to "double up" on the pain by ruminating on the discomfort. Ask yourself, *Will this matter in a year? Even in a month?*

# Week Three

Glance at the sun. See the moon and the stars.
Gaze at the beauty of earth's greenings.
Now, think.
What delight God gives to humankind
with all these things.

—HILDEGARD OF BINGEN

An early morning walk is a blessing for the whole day.

—HENRY DAVID THOREAU

One of our favorite family vacation activities is hiking. We can feast on all of the sensory gifts a new locale has to offer—the sounds of various birds calling, insects buzzing, frogs croaking, trees rustling, the smells of the native flowers, the sights of new plants and breathtaking vistas—all the while getting exercise and engaging in conversations with loved ones. It's the perfect combination.

Walking is a meditative practice in itself. It gets me into another world, feeding my spirit and my creativity. We are fortunate to live near a three-thousand-acre park that has many hiking trails. I take to these woods often, just to revel in the beauties and the sounds of nature. I see deer, hawks, frogs, turkeys, groundhogs, and an array of flora. Recently, we had some violent storms, which downed a host of trees. Seeing those trees lying flat on the ground, their leaves drying up for lack of nourishment, reminds me that all of life is tenuous. Nothing is guaranteed, but new life will spring up in the wake of destruction. These walking paths take on a new look every few weeks as we move from winter, to spring, to summer, to fall, and back again to winter. Everything changes, nothing stays the same, reminding me to be more at ease with the impermanence of life in general.

Two recent Stanford University studies provide more encouragement for walking. The researchers in one study showed that walking in a park soothes the mind and improves our mental health by changing how our brains work.[2] After a stroll through green space, study volunteers were happier, more attentive, and less apt to dwell on negative aspects of their lives. For urban residents, in particular, getting out into nature is an easy and effective way to improve their moods. Conservationist Rachel Carson acknowledged these positive effects, saying, "Those who contemplate the beauty of the earth find reserves of strength that will endure as long as life lasts."

Many recent studies have touted the health benefits of walking as well. Walking can help extend our lives while lowering our chances of developing Alzheimer's and other forms of dementia. It can reduce the pain of arthritic knees and the risk of several cancers, while improving survival rates for cancer patients. High insulin levels and inflammation seem to be controlled through exercise, too.

Walking also seems to work like antidepressant medications, increasing serotonin levels. We know our overall heart heath is improved by exercise, and the greater the intensity, the better. But even walking around the block or the mall is better than sitting at home. Danish philosopher Søren Kierkegaard advised: "Above all, do not lose your desire to walk. Every day I walk myself into a state of well-being and walk away from every illness. I have walked myself into my best thoughts."

## Putting the Wisdom into Practice

Take a walk—or a bike ride—a few days this week, preferably in the woods or in another natural spot near you. Notice one or two new features in the landscape that you've never observed before. Stop to gaze at tree bark, flowers, and the sky above. Leave your troubles at home and take in the natural world. Contemplate the miracles all around you. Remind yourself that it is a gift just to be alive.

# Week Four

Every breath we draw is a gift.... Every
moment of existence is a grace.
—THOMAS MERTON

A breath of love takes you all the way to infinity.
—RUMI

How often do you hear yourself saying one of these
phrases? "I can't catch my breath." "I need to take a
breather." "My schedule is suffocating." "I want some breathing room." We are unwittingly acknowledging the close connection between our breath and our spirit. Simply taking a
deep breath can bring awareness and attention to the here and
now, connecting our spirit to inner peace and calm, even in
the busiest of days.

Interestingly, "breath" and "spirit" are often linguistically
related. "Spirit" is derived from the Latin, *spirare*, meaning "to
breathe." In Greek, the word *pneuma* is translated as "breath"
or "spirit." And in Hebrew, the word *ruach* means "wind,"
"breath," or "spirit." So our language confirms what we already
surmise: healthy breath will lead us to a healthy spirit.

I recently had the opportunity to practice deep breathing
due to a household emergency. It was late in the afternoon,
Jack was out of town, and I was winding down my workday.
I loaded the dishwasher and turned it on. Less than a minute

later, I heard water gushing in our powder room. I raced into the room to see water pouring out of the cabinets and covering the floor. I ran around the house, shutting off the water valve, gathering towels to soak up the water, and draping plastic over our computer and printers one floor below the leak. Breathless, I called Jack to ask his advice on what to do next.

"Call the plumber," he said. Of course.

At this point I realized I was panting and needed to breathe. With a few deep inhales, I was able to bring a bit of space into my mind so I could think more clearly.

The breath is such a handy tool to have when little emergencies like this one strike. It's helpful to have a practice of deep breathing so we can access it on a moment's notice. Throughout the day, we can take a conscious breath every so often to remind us to come back to this moment and be present, or just to be grateful. Just one slow breath can defuse stressful situations (like a blown water pipe) and bring us out of our frantic, worrying mind. It calls us back from anxiety about the future or ruminating about the past.

There are many other reasons why deep breathing is good for us: it helps relieve pain and elevates our mood by slowing the release of cortisol and triggering the release of endorphins. It aids in weight loss by activating leptin, the hormone that helps inhibit hunger. Deep breathing can lower our blood pressure and reduce tension and stress by stimulating the parasympathetic nervous system. Many other bodily functions are improved as well, including the digestive, circulatory, cardiovascular, and immune systems. And lastly, breathing deeply strengthens the major organs of the body, resulting in increased energy and improved stamina.

Whew! That's quite a long list of benefits. Try beginning a deep breathing habit and begin experiencing those benefits today.

# Putting the Wisdom into Practice

This week, scatter several deep breathing pauses throughout each day. Pick a cue to help you remember, such as mealtime, tea or coffee time, bathroom breaks, opening and closing doors, traffic stops, waiting in line, or hanging up the phone. Any action you perform several times a day will work. Use the cue to bring your attention to your breath, and slowly inhale through your nose and then, even more slowly, exhale through your nose or mouth. Your body, mind, and spirit will thank you. (Perhaps coax a family member or two to join in, too!)

# SEPTEMBER

## Week One

To grow old is a glorious thing when one has
not unlearned what it means to begin.

—MARTIN BUBER

Continuity gives us roots; change gives us branches,
letting us stretch and grow and reach new heights.

—PAULINE R. KEZER

Oftentimes the month of September rolls around and I
find myself asking, *Where did the summer go? How can
it be September already?* School buses have returned, college
students are gone, and the light in the evening is diminish-
ing. Teachers and students alike hope to maximize classroom
achievement. It's a time of transition. During times like these,
our mindsets are crucial for determining whether we succeed
or fail in our new tasks.

Dr. Carol Dweck, a Stanford psychology professor, has
researched success and achievement. She teaches one of the

most popular courses on campus, "Self-Theories," in which she discusses two types of mindsets: fixed oriented and growth-oriented. If we have a fixed mindset, we believe that our intelligence and personality, along with other traits, are static, so we try to protect our image and tend to avoid challenges. When we see others succeed, we feel threatened instead of feeling happy. We tend to give up easily when faced with big obstacles and to discount the role that effort plays in our accomplishments. We also might ignore critical feedback that could help us become better in many ways. All of these fixed-mind characteristics conspire to create a deterministic worldview, thwarting our ability to achieve our full potential.

Growth-oriented folks, on the other hand, believe that intelligence can be developed, so we embrace challenges because we view them as essential to growth. We don't give up when we face setbacks because we believe that, with effort, strategy, and good instruction, we will learn from these difficulties. Dweck's research shows that failing and recovering are more valuable than sticking with what you already know. Growth-oriented people listen to criticism instead of feeling threatened, and we use this feedback to help us become better at what we do. Growth folks are also inspired by successful people. We welcome their presence. We want to absorb their wisdom. And finally, we view learning as a lifelong process, so ever-higher levels of achievement are possible. We wind up with a greater sense of free will and more openness about life in general.

As we transition from summer to fall, perhaps we might try a few of the growth mindset approaches. Then our growing older *will* be a "glorious thing"!

# Putting the Wisdom into Practice

Honestly appraise your mindset in a few areas of your life. Do you tend to have a growth or a fixed mindset? Is there a certain realm where you tend to be more fixed? If so, think of a few steps you can take to convert those into growth states. Keep working on being aware of the ways fixed attitudes creep into your life.

This research can be particularly helpful to young people and students. If you have a chance to share these findings with them (in a non-preachy way, of course), they might benefit from your words of encouragement. And if you're a parent, by all means let your kids fail a few times. Let them struggle and learn some grit. Model an openness to criticism and constructive comments. Remind them that we are all works in progress.

# Week Two

We are what we repeatedly do. Excellence,
therefore, is not an act, but a habit.

—ARISTOTLE

It's not enough to be busy. So are the ants.
The question is, what are we busy about?

—HENRY DAVID THOREAU

Someone once asked the Dalai Lama, "If you had only one word to describe the secret of happiness and of living a fulfilling life, what word would that be?" Without hesitating the Dalai Lama replied, "Routines." Routines help us organize our time and be more focused so that we can maximize our opportunities. They can simplify our lives by keeping us from having to make a multitude of decisions every time we awake.

The regularity that comes with the start of autumn is quite comforting to me. Perhaps that is because I loved school, and, as the wife of a teacher, I participate in beginning a new school year and another round of learning. Summer is the season for the imagination, but fall can be the season for putting those inspirations into action.

Is there a routine that you've abandoned that you'd like to recover? I find my practice of sitting and centering becomes less daily during the summer months, and I long for that regular appointment with silence. It could be as simple as preparing a cup of tea and sipping it for a few quiet moments before launching into an activity. As Thomas Merton reminds us in *Conjectures of a Guilty Bystander*, "To allow oneself to be carried away by a multitude of conflicting concerns, to surrender to too many demands, to commit oneself to too many projects, to want to help everyone in everything, is to succumb to violence."[1]

I don't think the Dalai Lama meant that we should take cover behind our routines and not allow life to stretch us. But if we jump from novelty to novelty, our souls fail to simmer in the lessons of the ordinary. Although January is the typical month to think about our habits and make changes in our routines to become healthier, maybe September can be another marker month. We might see that we need to tweak the new habits we started in January, or we may need to reset some of them and get back on track.

I've recently begun practicing the routine of the Ivy Lee Method, which recommends we do the most important thing first each day. It has pushed my productivity up another notch and maybe it can do the same for you. At the end of each day, write down the six most important things you need to accomplish the next day, in order from most important to least important. The next morning, work from top to bottom, finishing each item before beginning the next. At the end of your day, move any unfinished items to a new list for the next day.

# Putting the Wisdom into Practice

The biggest lesson from the Ivy Lee Method is to *do the most important thing first each day*. Just do that for the next seven days and see if your productivity goes up. And remember, the most important thing on your list may not have anything to do with "accomplishing." It may be meditating, calling a sick friend, or helping a neighbor. It's *your* list, so you decide what matters most to you. But this routine can help guide your spiritual life in the direction you want it to go.

# Week Three

We spend a long time wishing we
were elsewhere and otherwise.

—ROBERT FARRAR CAPON

The University of the Moment has been
built uniquely for each of us.

—ARCHBISHOP FULTON SHEEN

Some days don't go exactly as planned, or even close to it!
We had one of those days on a Saturday in September.
It started out with the racket of a jackhammer awakening us
early. I had wanted a few more minutes of shut-eye, but I knew
we had a great day ahead. Jack and I would explore a nearby
rails-to-trails path and then enjoy a few Gaelic bands at the
city's Irish festival that evening.

After lunch, we set out on the forty-five-minute car ride to
the trail. The ride quickly became complicated, due to detours,
traffic, and Google map errors. As the forty-five minutes grew
to ninety minutes, we kept telling ourselves to enjoy the beautiful weather and countryside. We knew if we focused on the
long travel time we'd taint the experience to come. So we
arrived at the parking lot described on the website in fairly
good spirits, ready to hit the trail. But where was the trailhead?
After an hour search (no kidding), a helpful ambulance driver
finally steered us to the unmarked path. So around the time I

expected to be completing the twenty-mile bike ride, I was just beginning. Oh, and the coffee shop near the parking lot where we stopped to get a dose of caffeine? It closed two minutes before we arrived.

The bike ride through the Pennsylvania woodlands was beautiful, as the leaves were beginning to change. The farther I pedaled, the more glorious the scenery, and somehow the trials and tribulations of getting there made the experience even sweeter. We didn't make it to the Irish festival due to our late start, but we did discover a new restaurant on our way home that we never would have visited had our plans not gone awry.

So, yes, it was one of those days, one filled with the realization that life is good even when the best-laid plans go haywire. That's a lesson I need to keep learning and relearning from the University of the Moment: every breath we take *is* a gift ... even through jackhammers and detours and getting lost and closed coffee shops!

## Putting the Wisdom into Practice

When your plans are derailed or unforeseen interruptions occur this week, remember to keep your eyes open for the good that can be found instead of focusing on that perfect plan. Our brains are wired to focus on danger and trouble, so we have to practice having a "Teflon brain" and letting it go. Then pay attention to the good. That's one of the keys to a life of happiness.

# Week Four

Your children are not your children.

They are the sons and daughters
of Life's longing for itself.

They come through you but not from you,

And though they are with you, yet
they belong not to you....

You are the bows from which your children
as living arrows are sent forth.

—KAHLIL GIBRAN

Having a child is to decide forever to have your
heart go walking around outside your body.

—ELIZABETH STONE

L etting go. Parents of college-bound children are practicing this in earnest this month. When our last child
boarded a plane for college, I was challenged to let go of the
daily exercises—some might say grind—of motherhood. Like
most moms, I'd been organizing, negotiating, planning, and
time-managing for many years. Who'd have thought I'd miss
that life? Certainly not the twenty-four-year-old engineer who
found herself pregnant only six months after her wedding. I
couldn't have predicted how much I would fall in love with
those babies, children, young adults. A door was closing and I

wanted to peek into the doorway one last time to savor the last moments of that life.

Letting go of that "mom hat" was tinged with anxiety, uncertainty, and a healthy dose of sadness. I asked myself, *Have I done enough for these three kids and imparted all of the lessons and tidbits of wisdom I'd hoped to give them?* Did other moms feel this way, too? If so, why hadn't anyone told me about this? How did I not get a notification, "Heartache ahead! Tread with caution!"

Once in a while, without warning, I would feel my heart open and tears would fill my eyes. I would miss this time in my life, all those tender, funny moments with our kids, driving in the car, attending concerts and cross-country meets and school meetings, talking late at night about dreams, doubts, aspirations, longings, disappointments. As Anne Lamott writes in *Operating Instructions*, "There really are places in the heart you don't even know exist until you love a child."[2] These three souls came into our lives depending on Jack and me for everything, and they now make their way fairly independently. The youthful energy that filled our home, our lives, and our hearts was so hard to relinquish.

After we dropped our son, Jackson, off at the Pittsburgh airport, sending him to Boston for his freshman year of college, Jack and I arrived home to a house draped in silence. I walked into the "kids'" bathroom to tidy up, caught sight of the empty toothbrush holder, and crumpled to the floor in an avalanche of tears. No sign of teenagers' paraphernalia: acne cream, hair gel, razors. It was completely cleaned out. No Kernion child would regularly use this bathroom again. I couldn't bring myself to look at our son's bed, the covers thrown back and Bear (his stuffed animal and childhood companion) in the middle of it. That same night, I heard a sound from downstairs and reflexively thought one of the kids had just arrived home before I realized my mistake. I'd have to retrain my mind to stop listening for the sounds of teenagers coming in the door after midnight.

Why did my heart ache so much during those first few days and weeks of empty-nesting? Half of my life had been spent raising children. I'd been happily immersed in leading them to their independence. And here they were, successfully launched into the world. I should be happy! But what helped me climb back out of the sadness was the deep gratitude I felt for all those years of parenting, and also for the newfound freedom I now experienced. Loving deeply doesn't mean "free from pain." I would do it all again, in a heartbeat.

# Putting the Wisdom into Practice

Have you experienced a major change in life that was tinged with both happy and sad emotions? How did you walk through the pain? Were friends and family there to help you? Was gratitude a part of that journey? If not, can you see that practicing thankfulness might be helpful in learning and growing and appreciating the experience? Writing about my experience helped me process the loss and move forward to new adventures. Perhaps give that a try, too.

# OCTOBER

# Week One

All change is a miracle to contemplate.

—HENRY DAVID THOREAU

There are only two ways to live your life. The
first is as though nothing is a miracle. The
second is as though everything is a miracle.

—ALBERT EINSTEIN

October is when the leaves begin to change in Pennsylvania. It's an "ordinary" spectacle I eagerly anticipate every year. In fact, I find it more and more amazing the older I get. The scientist in me enjoys pondering what is actually taking place in each leaf: chlorophyll is breaking down, causing the green color to disappear. As the green fades away, the yellows and oranges appear. These pigments have been present all along, but were masked by the green. When about half of the chlorophyll is degraded, red pigments are synthesized and we are treated to another layer of beautiful colors. The resulting kaleidoscope, multiplied a hundredfold, graces the hillsides all around us. I find this amazing and incredible and miraculous. How else to see it?

Speaking of seeing things, I have two friends, José and William, who are bringing new perspectives to our lives. They are sixteen-year-old immigrants who made the harrowing trip by themselves from Guatemala, braving rain, hunger, and danger I can't comprehend—all for the chance at a better life. We don't know if they will be allowed to stay, but they are joyful, kind, and thankful for the simplest things. Having their fresh eyes on our world is illuminating. On a trip to the mall, they point out every Halloween decoration ("More!?" they exclaim. "Yes," I reply. "We overdo it here, don't we?") and find the escalator a terribly exciting experience—they film themselves as they ride it up, up, up. Visiting the sporting goods store reveals the wonders of treadmills and bowling balls. The grocery store is a fantasyland, with much of the food completely foreign to them. Even our backyard is a surprise to them: "This is all *yours*?" Their joy and wonder at the common and ordinary give us pause. I'll never again look at a bowling ball—or my backyard—in the same way.

José and William are walking in hope. They hope for a better education; a safer, longer life; and more opportunities to learn and grow. My hope is to try to live each day with the joy and knowledge that everything is a miracle, as they do. The glorious, changing leaves around us can be our daily reminders.

# Putting the Wisdom into Practice

There are ordinary wonders—miracles, really—everywhere around us. We just need to remember to pause and take some time to really *see* them. Each day this week, look around and find at least one ordinary wonder that you may have overlooked in the past. You might choose the tree outside your window, the stove that cooks your food, or, like José and William, an escalator. Focus your attention on that wonder, think about its origin, evolution, and uses, and be grateful for the ways it is a miracle. To live with the recognition of all of those ordinary miracles is to live with great joy.

# Week Two

Thanks to the human heart by which we live,
Thanks to its tenderness, its joys, and fears.

—WILLIAM WORDSWORTH

There is no charm equal to tenderness of heart.

—JANE AUSTEN

One weekend, while at the grocery store with my grand-daughter Morgan, I noticed twenty or so ShopRite employees standing around the checkout lanes, not doing anything in particular. It seemed rather odd, but when I noticed a few of them chatting with a young woman in military fatigues, I thought perhaps they were going to honor a veteran or something like that. I didn't give it much thought and proceeded to the line, where Morgan and I began softly singing a few songs to pass the time. All of a sudden, applause erupted and we looked over to see the young woman hugging an older woman in a ShopRite uniform. They were both crying and hugging each other. I discovered that the young military member had surprised her mom by coming home while she was working. I couldn't help but cry as I took in this scene of tenderness and unbridled joy. I glanced around the checkout area and heard an older woman saying, "We're all crying and we don't even know who these people are. But it's so moving, isn't it?" Indeed it was. We were experiencing the deep love between a mother and daughter, captured in a moment of intense euphoria and relief. Glimpsing the beauty and splendor of the human heart, I couldn't help but think of my own daughters, the love I have for them, and how proud I am of the mothers they have become.

Earlier that week, Morgan and I were in the Pittsburgh airport, waiting to board a midday commuter flight to Newark, New Jersey. We took our spot in "Group 4" at the United gate, surrounded by Very Serious Businesspeople, no one making eye contact, everyone busy on their phones or computers. Morgan wrapped her arms around my legs and began singing "Twinkle, Twinkle Little Star" at the top of her two-year-old lungs. By the end of the first few lines, the Serious People in Suits couldn't ignore the little strawberry-blond balladeer, and one by one turned around and smiled at us. But Morgan was completely oblivious of the attention, singing confidently at a slow, deliberate pace, loud as can be, breaking the poker-faced atmosphere one note at a time with her sweet song. When she was finished, a few people broke into enthusiastic applause, and nearly everyone smiled broadly as they turned and acknowledged her performance.

About ninety minutes later we landed and Morgan and I deplaned and began walking toward baggage claim. One of the Serious People passed us, turned around, took out his earphones, and asked Morgan, "Did you see any stars on the flight?" "I saw clouds," replied Morgan. What I saw was some sunshine breaking through, brought by a two-year-old to a group rather in need of some lightheartedness that afternoon.

# Putting the Wisdom into Practice

These two events remind me to continue trying to live by the heart, to be thankful for "its tenderness, its joys, and fears." Isn't that really what life is all about? I shouldn't worry about being embarrassed or being seen as too sappy, too forgiving, too silly. Even though these qualities aren't always encouraged, it's never too late to nourish their development.

Perhaps you can try to be a bit more gentle than usual with people this week: family, friends, coworkers, and neighbors. Give them the benefit of the doubt, wrap them in a little more love, and keep in mind that each person's heart can be opened wider with just a little bit of encouragement. As you express your vulnerability and tenderness, you invite others to do the same.

# Week Three

In the sweet territory of silence we touch the
mystery ... the place where we can connect with
the deep knowing, to the deep wisdom way.

—ANGELES ARRIEN

[People] need enough silence and solitude
in their lives to enable the deep inner voice
of their own true self to be heard.

—THOMAS MERTON

The trick to much in our spiritual lives is *remembering*, and that's why I find silence so necessary. In *Amazing Grace*, best-selling novelist and poet Kathleen Norris shares wisdom from a child who mused, "Silence reminds me to take my soul with me wherever I go."[1]

There is a well-known Hasidic story that speaks to our sense of place and its deeper meanings for our spiritual lives.

The child of a rabbi used to wander in the woods. At first his father let him wander, but after a while he grew concerned. The woods were dangerous. The father wasn't sure what lurked there.

He decided to discuss the matter with his son. One day, he took him aside and said, "You know, I have noticed that each day you walk in the woods. I wonder, why do you go there?"

The boy said, "I go there to find God."

"That is a very good thing," the father replied gently. "I am glad you are searching for God. But my child, don't you know that God is the same everywhere?"

"Yes," the boy answered, "but I'm not."

I understand the boy's perspective. Every so often, I head to a monastery or retreat center for a few days of reflection. Certain places—call them "holy" or "sacred" or simply "inspiring"—ground me like no others. I see things in new ways. I remember, again, the essentials of life. I will breathe and walk and listen and observe ... in gratitude. That's all. Sure, I don't have to go anywhere to do those things. But I go to the monastery because, as this little boy says, I am not the same everywhere.

Some monasteries practice bowing to another person upon greeting them or saying good-bye. In this simple act we pause to honor the person in front of us, to acknowledge their humanity, their dignity. We entered into this practice on a family trip to Thailand several years ago, adopting the local custom, and it was an unexpected gift. We were so sad to leave the custom at the trip's end.

Mister Rogers said that the act of bowing is an acknowledgment of the eternal in our neighbor. "You see," he says, "I believe that appreciation is a holy thing, that when we look for what's best in the person we happen to be with at the moment, we're doing what God does." In loving and appreciating our neighbor, we're participating in something truly sacred.

The practice of bowing reminds us to look for the sacred in the other person. Bowing creates a moment of silence in which we have the space to remember what is holy in others, what is sacred in ourselves, what is most meaningful in our connections with others. We honor those sacred connections with a bow, looking for the best in our neighbor, for *that* is the eternal.

# Putting the Wisdom into Practice

Is it possible to bow a bit to every person you meet this week? Maybe a full-out bow isn't appropriate, but try a head nod or even just a chin dip. Whether you can acknowledge it physically or not, bring your attention to the eternal in each person you greet, and look for the best in her.

# Week Four

The art of living lies in a fine mingling
of letting go and holding on.

—HAVELOCK ELLIS

The only way to make sense out of change is to
plunge into it, move with it, and join the dance.

—ALAN WATTS

One beautiful autumn day, my friendly bank teller looked somewhat melancholy, so I asked her if she was okay. Mary Lynn responded, "It's that time of year, Anne. I know the leaves are beautiful and the cool air is refreshing, but I know what's coming and I'm not looking forward to it." We talked about the shortening days, the cooler temperatures, and how it's not always easy to adjust to the change from fall to winter.

That conversation got me thinking about change, of letting go and holding on, and accepting and allowing. Often it's not the change itself that is difficult. We just get comfortable with our lives and don't want things to be altered in any way. It's hard to think about the "what ifs." *What if my situation changes and it's more demanding? What if I don't like the new boss, new neighborhood, new coworker, new dynamic, new school?*

But if we can become comfortable with change, we can find peace and even joy in it. How can we let go of the fear of the unknown and stop fighting what the future may hold? Here are several suggestions:

1. Try to view change as an opportunity. New doors have opened up for you and it might—just might—be wonderful.

2. Allow things to change. Accept what *is*. Do you want to look back on these years and realize you wasted precious days wishing you were elsewhere and otherwise?

3. Become aware of your clinging. What are you holding on to when you feel fear, uncertainty, or pain? Often it's just an idea or an image, not reality.

4. See the mental energy it takes to cling. Once you see your clinging more clearly, you see the pain that results from it. Everything you cling to has a downside.

5. Experience joy in the unknown. There are endless possibilities in new experiences, new friends, a new path. And that can be joyful.

## Putting the Wisdom into Practice

This week, notice when you are resisting a change in your life. Meditation is a great tool for practicing letting go, and it also increases our ability to be attentive and awake. As we sit in meditation, we let go of our thoughts, they come back, we let go again—over and over. Our mind will wander, and when we notice it, we come back to focus. We aim to stay present to whatever is arising, without reacting further. The key is to be gentle with yourself and carry on. Try these suggestions:

1. Commit to sitting for just a minute or two each day. That way you can't make the excuse that you don't have the time.
2. Find a quiet place to sit comfortably, with a straight spine. Rest your hands on your lap. Gently close your eyes and take a few cleansing breaths.
3. Let your breath be slow and deep.
4. Disengage from your thoughts and feelings using one of the methods below:
   - Count your breath, up to ten. Repeat. When you get sidetracked by thoughts, just come back to one and start again.
   - Repeat a sacred word or phrase every breath or two.
   - Do a slow body scan, starting with your head and working down to your toes.

When the time is over, gently open your eyes and return to the "doing" part of your day, with a calm and relaxed mind. As you continue this practice throughout your days, you will find that you experience your emotions and let them flow through you instead of them taking over.

# NOVEMBER

## Week One

We live our lives forward but
understand them backward.

—SØREN KIERKEGAARD

When your mother asks, "Do you want a piece of
advice?" it is a mere formality. It doesn't matter if
you answer yes or no. You're going to get it anyway.

—ERMA BOMBECK

If you could go back several decades, what advice would you
give your younger self? What would you tell her to ease her
journey and help her fully appreciate the path ahead? Here's
what I wish my younger self had known:

1. It'll be okay if everyone doesn't like you. You can twist
   yourself in knots trying to please everyone, and you
   still won't succeed. (If only I'd listened to my dad on
   that one!)

2. You'll find your direction. Don't fret about it. And the side trips might teach and assist in ways you can't imagine.

3. Be gentle and compassionate with yourself. Treat yourself with the same kindness you would extend to your friends.

4. Go after that new guy, Jack, in your singing group. (I was in love with him months before I could muster up the courage to tell him. And he felt the same way, but since I was committed to becoming a missionary, he didn't want to tell me either. Geesh!)

5. Those long, tiring days with your little ones will be over before you blink. Don't wish even one of them away.

6. The little moments in life are the important ones. Breathe deeply and enjoy them.

7. Give yourself a break when you make a mistake. None of us is perfect, so stop expecting it from yourself. As American actress Tallulah Bankhead said, "If I had to live my life again, I'd make the same mistakes, only sooner." Forgive yourself like you do others.

8. Try an activity out of your comfort zone once in a while. You're most likely to regret what you didn't do, not what you did.

9. You don't need to prove yourself to anyone. Never think, *I'll be worthy when/if I* _____.

10. Hard work pays off. You don't have to be the best at anything to be successful. Just keep working and enjoy the ride.

11. Risk being tender and compassionate. Wear your heart on your sleeve sometimes, even when it feels uncomfortable.

12. When people are harsh, insensitive, or thoughtless, it's not about you. They are probably carrying a burden. Let it go.

13. Life is shorter than you think. Be grateful every day.

14. All of the habits and routines you begin in your early years will have consequences in your later years, for better or for worse. Choose wisely.

15. Did I mention that guy Jack? You'll never regret getting to know him.

## Putting the Wisdom into Practice

Do any of these pieces of advice ring true for you? What guidance would you give your younger self? Ponder those thoughts this week and maybe write a few down. If you have children, share your thoughts with them. Or save them to include with their holiday gifts. Your struggles and hard-won life lessons can be a source of wisdom for others.

# Week Two

If we walk in hope, we have joy in our
hearts. Let us be lights of hope.

—POPE FRANCIS

For all that has been, Thank you.
For all that is to come, Yes.

—DAG HAMMARSKJÖLD

Several Sunday nights throughout the year, I gather with my
Renew group to discuss inspirational readings. We listen to
one another, encourage each other, rejoice at good news, and
comfort each other during difficult times. For about a decade
now, I've been inspired by their lives, their examples, and their
collective strength. Because most of the members are five to
twenty years older than me, they sometimes confront circumstances that have yet to appear in my life. I learn much from
how they handle these ups and downs and I feel fortunate to
have such wisdom close at hand.

One of the most profound lessons I've learned from these
older friends is to live in hope. Their attitude is born of years
of experience, faith, and perseverance. Our oldest member,
Rose Marie, lost her husband several years ago. He was our
beloved leader and we all still miss him. But even in her loss,
Rose Marie continues to live life with a deep serenity and joy.
She is grateful for the years past and welcomes each new day

with a determined "Yes." She is also one of the most prolific letter writers I know, sending carefully crafted notes to authority figures and ordinary folks alike. She affirms and encourages, but also prods and questions. When she disagrees with a community or religious leader, she strives to enter a dialogue and discover common ground. And she doesn't waver in her hope and trust that every action we take can make a difference. Her tenacity, combined with utmost gentleness, teaches me to see possibility in disagreement.

I am so grateful to have Rose Marie's hopeful, joyful light in my life. Since November is the month of Thanksgiving, I intend to thank her and others who have guided, supported, and mentored me along the way. They are my lights of hope.

## Putting the Wisdom into Practice

First, think of several people who have been lights of hope in your life. Set aside a few moments to write a note of gratitude to each one, preferably on paper or in a card, so they can save it. What joy they will feel upon receiving and reading your thoughts! Second, reflect on the quality of hope in your life. Do you express hope and nurture it in your activities and speech? Be aware of how you walk in hope this week.

# Week Three

Seeing. We might say that the whole
of life lies in that verb.

—PIERRE TEILHARD DE CHARDIN

Our perennial spiritual task is to look at things
familiar until they become unfamiliar again.

—G. K. CHESTERTON

While leading a weekend retreat, I instructed the attendees to spend some time walking around the grounds observing nature, taking in details that might be missed at just a glance. Our Saturday afternoon topic was how vital the art of looking—really looking—is to our spirituality and creativity. We so rarely spend time just stopping and observing the everyday things and people around us. If we don't spend time being still, as the psalmist recommends, we certainly won't be in any frame of mind to truly see the gifts everywhere. And if we don't see the gifts that sit right in front of our eyes, we miss some of the most poignant blessings in our lives. As priest and theologian John Shea notes, "The spiritual life is, at root, a matter of seeing."

I reminded the retreatants that we cannot be creative if we don't invest at least a small bit of time looking around, taking in the nuances of our landscapes: landscapes that include trees, hills, flowers, rocks, leaves, stars, clouds, birds, berries, the eyes of our friends, the faces of our family members, the smiles of our coworkers. The bark of a tree has lines and textures we overlook if we don't spend time really *seeing* it. How often do we even notice the changing faces of our friends and family? Ignatius of Loyola reminds us to "find God in all things." We certainly can't find God in *any* thing if our eyes aren't open to all the subtle wonders life offers us—*every single day*.

If we can learn to be seers—seers of blessings, seers of loved ones, seers of good deeds and good intentions, seers of ordinary gifts and extraordinary ones, too—we will be filled to the brim with gratitude and more aware of the gift of love in our lives. Those faces gathered around the Thanksgiving table are gifts, ones that may or may not be there again next year. So take a good look. Really notice their faces, their smiles, their expressions, and yes, even their wrinkles, crooked teeth, and gray hair.

To truly see others is to honor and appreciate them as other souls on the journey. If we can do that, our tables will certainly be filled with gratitude and thanksgiving.

# Putting the Wisdom into Practice

We often walk around half-blind to what's in front of us. So let's open our eyes and see! What colors are present at sunset, now that winter is approaching? What are your family and coworkers conveying nonverbally—joy, despair, hope, sorrow, anxiety? Look up and see the stars and moon each night this week. There is so much to take in, if only we take the time.

# Week Four

A self that goes on changing is a
self that goes on living.

—VIRGINIA WOOLF

Go confidently in the direction of your
dreams. Live the life you have imagined.

—HENRY DAVID THOREAU

With an empty house after our last child left for college,
I knew I couldn't cling to my old identity as a mother
of teenagers. It wasn't easy to let go of that. I had a job I loved,
but friends advised waiting out this apprehensiveness at being
an empty nester: *Don't take on any new projects for one year. Ask
yourself what you really want to do with your time, what activities
bring you joy and can use your unique gifts.*

Neuroscience research suggests that we can keep our brains
healthier and happier if we continue to try novel things, learn
new skills, and take on interesting challenges. So when we
reach a juncture in life, it's important to consider opportunities
that will stretch us and pull us into new arenas.

The Hindu wisdom on the three stages of life is helpful to
ponder. During the first stage, the "student" stage, our main
responsibility is to learn as much as possible: hone our char-
acter, learn good habits, and acquire skills that will serve us

throughout our life span. The second stage, beginning with marriage, is the stage when human longings are fulfilled: pleasure through marriage and family; success through vocation and career; duty through community involvement.

As we move throughout the second stage, which takes a few decades, our energy and excitement begin to wane a bit. Career and duty begin to be less interesting and more repetitious, and the third stage of life begins. This is an exciting stage, too, for we can explore what life is all about, what matters most to us, and who we truly are. It is the time of self-discovery and time to figure out—if we haven't already—a philosophy of life. And then we are at peace, content with whatever life has to offer, living fully in the present, without worry or care.

As a new empty nester, I was living on the cusp of stages two and three, letting ideas ferment and living with the uncomfortable nature of "in between" time. Two recommendations from neuroscience were particularly helpful: if we commit to a goal and find ways to serve others, we will increase our happiness. So I asked myself a few questions: What dreams and goals did I have in my early twenties that were put on hold to raise our family? Could I combine these interests and serve others, too? Pondering those questions allowed me to welcome two new pursuits, teaching yoga and giving presentations on spirituality, bringing much new joy to my life.

As Christian theologian G. K. Chesterton observed, "There is one thing which gives radiance to everything. It is the idea of something around the corner."

# Putting the Wisdom into Practice

We are always coming upon junctures, big and small, that give us opportunities to make changes. What is something you haven't taken time to develop and nurture before? What excites you? What talents would you enjoy sharing with others? What new direction could you take to make the world a better place? "Listen to life with an open heart," St. Benedict reminds us. There are people everywhere who are in need, and what great joy we find in serving others with our unique talents.

# DECEMBER

## Week One

Try pausing right before and right after
undertaking a new action. Even something simple
like putting a key in a lock to open a door.

—DAVID STEINDL-RAST

Discipline means to prevent everything in your life
from being filled up…. In the spiritual life, discipline
means to create that space in which something can
happen that you hadn't planned or counted on.

—HENRI NOUWEN

We have officially entered the season of "have to," as in,
I *have to* shop for gifts, I *have to* wrap presents, I *have
to* decorate the house, I *have to* address my Christmas cards, I
*have to* call Aunt Mildred about the holiday menu. All of these
*have to*'s can add up to a pile of stress. And stress takes away
from our enjoyment of all the lovely gifts the holidays bring.

What if we replaced the words *have to* with *get to*? I *get to* shop for gifts, I *get to* wrap presents, I *get to* decorate the house, I *get to* call Aunt Mildred. This simple language substitution transforms the list from stress-inducing to being filled with appreciation for the opportunity to complete the tasks at hand. We can step back and consider all of the people who would be thrilled to have money to buy gifts, to have loved ones for whom they wrap presents, to have a house to decorate, to have loved ones nearby.

We don't want to think of holiday duties as burdens, but when our list grows too long and time grows too short, that's what it feels like. We might consider saying no to a few responsibilities, or asking ourselves, *Is this necessary?* For about ten years now, I haven't mailed my Christmas cards before the 25th. I asked myself, *Do my friends and family really care if they receive them on the 28th instead of the 24th? Or to be honest, even January 8th?* (I have a good excuse. My mom said Christmas should be celebrated until Epiphany.) *Voilà!* That item is off my Christmas "to-do" list and I enjoy the task so much more now. We also no longer decorate the outside of the house with lights, replacing them with a simple wreath on the front door. Who says I have to decorate when no one in our family will be here to see it?

Perhaps you can take a look at your list of *have to*'s and eliminate the unnecessary ones. Think about the ones that remain in a new way: turn the *have to*'s into *get to*'s. We might discover, as Julian of Norwich said, "The fullness of joy is to behold God in everything." Even in—particularly in—holiday preparations.

# Putting the Wisdom into Practice

Here we go! The holidays are here, and even if you've simplified your preparations, you are likely still cleaning and planning and rushing and shopping and baking and wrapping. Hopefully you can carve out some time to taste silence and stillness. Perhaps walk outside and gaze at the night sky and stars. It only takes a few brief moments, but the heavens above can remind us of how inconsequential our to-do lists are in the scheme of things. And you give yourself a little gift of calm. Taking a few moments like this allows us to be more open and awake to all the gifts—and challenges—the holiday celebrations can offer us. If you've succeeded in changing your mindset to one of gratitude, your centered presence can be a wonderful gift to those around you who are overwhelmed by the duties of the season.

# Week Two

Something precious is lost if we rush headlong into
the details of life without pausing for a moment to pay
homage to the mystery of life and the gift of another day.
—KENT NERBURN

Impatience turns a very short time into a long one.
—TERESA OF ÁVILA

It is a serious challenge to be patient in the days before Christmas. Most of us have long lists of things to do, those details of life that claim our minutes and hours this time of year. I truly want to keep calm and breathe deeply when I find myself getting a little harried. But boy, that is not easy to remember. One mid-December day, I dropped by my printer to pick up a small job, an errand that should take no more than ten or fifteen minutes. The owner asked if we could talk for a few minutes about pricing, which I should have known wouldn't take just a few minutes, but I agreed. Let's just say that it didn't proceed smoothly. There were interruptions at every turn—phone calls, deliveries, machine malfunctions, employee questions—and my patience wore thinner and thinner as I waited at the counter, thinking about all the items I wasn't crossing off today's list.

Unfortunately, patience is not one of my strong suits. I'm realizing more and more that impatience robs me of awareness, tranquillity, and the gift of presence. We (I) exhibit all sorts of behaviors when we're impatient: we tap our fingers, shift side to side, jiggle our legs, twirl our hair, bite our nails, and "harrumph." We want time to speed up so we can get on to the next thing. But this impatience of ours doesn't make anything happen any faster. It just makes us miserable.

Perhaps I'll just offer the advice I need to hear myself in the last days of the year, and see if it applies to you, too: "Pause for a moment or two or three each day to pay homage to this wondrous Mystery of Life. Take a deep breath when you realize you are exhibiting impatient behavior." Then perhaps I'll avoid rushing and savor the gift of this day, this one precious day that is given to us, this one day that will never come again.

# Putting the Wisdom into Practice

December is the granddaddy of all months to help us become aware of our impatient tendencies. Notice when you begin fidgeting or using phrases like, "What's taking so long?" "Where is the salesperson?" "Why is this line moving so slowly?" These can be cues to bring our attention to the moment, to realize when we're not attending to the gift of this day. The sooner we can catch ourselves, the less misery we will experience. Since most of the time we can't do anything about the situation causing our impatience, giving our energy to it is a waste of resources and drains the joy out of life. Catch yourself and use the time to practice mindfulness and gratitude.

And give your gift of patience to another. Say, "Take your time. I'm not in a hurry" to someone who is late meeting you or is ahead of you at the checkout line, struggling to pack her groceries quickly. These words let the other person relax and de-stress for a few seconds. What a gift that can be in this busy season!

# Week Three

Look at how a single candle can both
defy and define the darkness.

—ANNE FRANK

Embrace the present moment as an
ever-flowing source of holiness.

—JEAN-PIERRE DE CAUSSADE

My childhood memories of the season of Advent are quite vivid: lighting purple and rose candles on the Advent wreaths, opening the miniature doors of Advent calendars with my siblings and fighting over whose turn it was. We celebrated the feast of St. Nicholas on December 6, receiving Reese's peanut butter cups and big apples in our shoes.

In the Catholic world of my childhood, Advent candles reminded me to be patient. The gifts and goodies of Christmas were coming, but I needed to wait calmly for them. Christmas wasn't going to come until after that fourth candle was lit and all the doors on the Advent calendar were open. I marked the season's progress by the candles. In my child's mind, candlelight meant pausing and not rushing ahead too quickly to the end of the season.

Now, as an adult, candlelight continues to remind me to be patient and still. Our energy might begin to sag as winter sets in, and the ritual of candlelighting can provide a lift to our spirits. It can bring our attention back to *this* moment, so our minds aren't jumping around as they can easily do in December. Observing candlelight for a little pause in our day can bring awareness to "the sacrament of the present moment," as eighteenth-century Jesuit priest Jean-Pierre de Caussade called it. We can be present to Life, remembering to be grateful for warmth, light, and everyday blessings.

Brother David Steindl-Rast says this about the ritual of candlelighting:

> To light a candle by myself is one of my favorite prayers. The very act of lighting the candle is prayer. There is the sound of striking the match, the whiff of smoke after blowing it out, the way the flame flares up and then sinks … All this and the darkness beyond my small circle of light is prayer."

# Putting the Wisdom into Practice

As the winter solstice nears, dark nights envelop us and invite introspection. Light a candle or two this week, mindfully and deliberately. Then sit for a moment and try a simple breathing exercise: Breathe in as you count to four; exhale as you count to six. Focus on the breath, on the cool air entering your nostrils, the warm air leaving. Four counts in, six counts out. Watch the flame dance, taking in the fragrance as the wax slowly melts. Let this be a meditation and prayer to still your spirit and bring peace to you as you prepare for the holiday festivities.

# Week Four

One by one, O God, I see and I love
all those you have given me
to charm and sustain my life.
—PIERRE TEILHARD DE CHARDIN

It is a fine seasoning for joy to think of those we love.
—MOLIÈRE

Christmas and holiday cards are rolling in, reminding us how many wonderful people grace our lives. New friends, old friends, family near and far. We see pictures of growing children, babies, young adults, and newlyweds, calling to mind the many seasons of life. Cards with beautiful messages of hope, gratitude, love, unity, and goodness reflect the senders' wishes for us and the world at large. I can't help but be filled with joy when I open each card, knowing someone has thought of our family again this year. I am prompted to think of Thomas Merton's wise words, "Life is this simple: we are living in a world that is absolutely transparent and the divine is shining through it all the time."

As philosopher Howard Thurman recounts, "I remember in gratitude … the beautiful things I have seen, heard and felt, many of which came unheralded into my path, warming my heart and rejoicing my spirit."

# Putting the Wisdom into Practice

Everything we do is a practice. *How* we go about doing things is a practice. Open each card with care. Look at the envelope and handwriting, the stamp that was chosen for the card. Practice gratitude, practice paying attention, practice doing good deeds, practice breathing slowly when life throws you a curveball. We count our blessings and use our daily tasks to remind us to be present and awake.

# ADDITIONAL WEEKS TO FILL OUT THE YEAR

 ## Week One

Speak a kind word …. You can make at
least one person happy every day.

—LAWRENCE G. LOVASIK

I can live for two months on a good compliment.

—MARK TWAIN

Isn't it amazing how one compliment can make our day infinitely brighter? I sometimes smile inside all day long after receiving one.

Twelfth-century Christian mystic Hildegard of Bingen expressed the idea of interconnectedness in her writings and paintings. She advocated for vitality, goodness, and right relationships with everything. One way we can promote this interconnectedness and goodness is to affirm others around us.

JoAnn, a woman at my gym, nurtures connection at every turn. I call her our Homecoming Queen. She enters each class with a smile on her face, greeting everyone, and then hands out affirmations like it's her job. "Oh, Sally, your haircut looks great." "Sue, we've missed you! Have you been away?" "Oh, Terry, did I ever tell you that you have a beautiful smile?" On and on it goes. Who doesn't want to be around that vitality and energy? And JoAnn does this without a whiff of pretension. She is a walking ambassador of interconnectedness.

How do we foster that type of relationship building? If we train ourselves to look for the positive traits in others, we find that the more we look, the more we see. Neuroscience research confirms this, too.

If you admire another person, by all means, tell them! Try to discover one good characteristic in every person you meet. It might be a challenge for some folks, but keep looking. When you find a positive attribute, you can give an honest compliment. And it's always more meaningful to compliment a personal quality rather than something superficial like physical appearance. You'll create a deeper connection with the other person and build your self-esteem and happiness, too. Searching for the good in others will also derail the tendency to criticize those who bug you. Yes, it's hard, I know. But criticism hinders connection. Go for the positive, and you'll see your relationships gain warmth and intimacy. As Francis of Assisi said, "It is in giving that we receive."

How do we start a complimenting practice?

1. Be genuine and specific. Begin with, "I was so touched by the way you ..." Center your compliments around something that affected you.

2. Be brief and give freely. "You were so patient with that customer." You don't have to give a speech. Simple compliments will be more readily remembered. Also, don't expect the recipient to respond with a compliment. We don't praise others so they will praise us in return.

3. Take a risk. "You worked really hard to raise those great kids." I find it easy to compliment family, but I'm more apprehensive with those I don't know as well. I don't want to be taken the wrong way, like I'm joking or being sarcastic. But if I am earnest and the compliment is genuine, the recipient will know I'm sincere. Every time I've done this, I've received a smile and a big "thank you." It really is easy to spread the love once we overcome our discomfort.

4. Don't wait for the perfect moment to give a compliment. For the recipient, it's always the perfect time.

# Putting the Wisdom into Practice

This week, look for opportunities to compliment those around you. Start small, perhaps with one easy compliment, and build up to one or two a day. Begin by complimenting a family member or close friend and work up to complimenting a personal quality you notice in an acquaintance. No matter where you go, be authentic in appreciating others. You'll spread cheer and build deeper connections and a wholehearted appreciation for life.

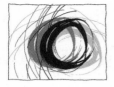

# Week Two

What a wonderful life I've had! I only
wish I'd realized it sooner.

—SIDONIE GABRIELLE COLETTE

I don't want to get to the end of my life and
find that I have lived just the length of it. I
want to have lived the width of it as well.

—DIANE ACKERMAN

When Elizabeth, Jackson, and my greeting card business
were all young and growing, we would often drop by
the Sisters of Mercy Motherhouse and visit our favorite sisters,
several of whom were elderly but still quite sharp. The kids
enjoyed eating ice cream and cookies in the cafeteria, skipping
through the cavernous hallways of the convent, and basking in
all of the attention they received from the sisters. I was simply
grateful to take part in an adult conversation with friends.

One of our favorite sisters was Sister Emmanuel Hampsey,
a woman of immense joy and grace, who had a degenerative
bone disease that caused her to have a severe hunch. We would
kneel down below her face to see her eyes. Elizabeth and Jackson were drawn to the sweet voice and gentle demeanor of this
tiny but luminous woman.

When Sister Emmanuel died, Elizabeth was devastated. She
asked if she could attend the wake with me, and Jack and I

decided it might be good for her to hear stories of Emmanuel and help her realize that she was indeed gone. So we said, "Sure, you can go." Hearing this, Elizabeth jumped up, put on her coat, and grabbed an empty green bean can from the counter as she dashed out the door. A few minutes later, she returned with the can filled with dirt and grass, saying, "I'm going to give this to Emmanuel so she can be buried with some real grass. There weren't any flowers outside, but she would like this." She then ran to her room and came back with a pencil and torn piece of paper, and wrote these words: "Emmanuel, your [sic] my best friend. I am going to miss you. Love, Elizabeth."

*Oh my*, I thought. *How am I going to tell her that she can't give an old can filled with dirt and grass to Sister Emmanuel's family?* This news would not be taken lightly, for even at the age of five, Elizabeth heard the word "no" as an invitation to begin negotiations. I pondered how to handle this situation as we ate dinner, got dressed up, and headed to the Mercy Motherhouse, Elizabeth cradling her can of dirt and grass. I tried to gently inform her that most people gave flowers to the family, and maybe she should leave the can in the car. "No," she said firmly. "Emmanuel would like that I picked something for her all by myself. I'm bringing this to her." She was so confident about this can of grass, and I couldn't really think of a good reason why she shouldn't give this gift to Emmanuel's family, except for the fact that it might be a little, well, a lot, embarrassing. So we arrived at the motherhouse and stood in a long line to greet the family. When we finally reached Emmanuel's niece, "Winkie" (who had an uncanny resemblance to Emmanuel, both in appearance and in manner), Elizabeth handed the can to her and said she wanted Sister Emmanuel to have it. To my astonishment, Winkie accepted the gift as though it were the most precious thing she had ever received, and gently placed it inside the casket.

Winkie wrote to Elizabeth a few weeks later, expressing her thanks for the thoughtful gift and note she'd brought for Emmanuel. A few months after that, when she discovered Elizabeth loved playing "tea party," Winkie sent her Emmanuel's prized tea set. And although Winkie lived in Baltimore, four and a half hours away by car, we visited her several times, exchanging letters frequently between visits. Winkie became a light and guide in Elizabeth's life, even serving as her confirmation sponsor. Years later, Elizabeth flew with her new fiancé from Chicago to Baltimore so Winkie could meet Brady, and, I think, solicit her blessing on their union.

Winkie's kind, supportive, and gentle spirit has touched our lives for over two decades now, and she is a treasured friend. We all enjoy recounting the evening we met, chuckling about that can of grass and dirt, remembering how the unvarnished love of a child brought us together. Teresa of Ávila reminds us that "the important thing is not to think much but to love much; and so do that which best stirs you to love." I am relieved that my parental embarrassment didn't thwart the beauty of that initial meeting. If it had, we would have missed the loving relationship we now experience with this special woman, whom I continue to visit on yearly business trips to Baltimore. Elizabeth and I also keep up our correspondence with Winkie the old-fashioned way, through cards and letters, embodying the words of poet John Donne: "Letters mingle souls; for thus friends absent speak."

# Putting the Wisdom into Practice

This week, try bringing more openness and less protectiveness to your daily encounters with others. Be attentive to the moments when pride or embarrassment works its way into your conversation or decision making. Try to show more honesty and vulnerability to others, letting down your guard a bit more than might be comfortable. "Leaning into the discomfort of vulnerability teaches us how to live with joy, gratitude and grace," writes Brené Brown in *The Gifts of Imperfection*.[1] If you have little ones in your life, watch how freely they interact with others. They can be excellent guides for us.

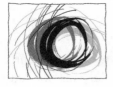

# Week Three

Words are the most powerful force available to
humanity. We can use this force constructively
with words of encouragement, or destructively
with words of despair. Words have energy and
power to help and heal, or to hurt and humiliate.

—YEHUDA BERG

Words are powerful. Be careful how you use them
because once you have pronounced them, you
cannot remove the scar they leave behind.

—VASHTI QUIROZ-VEGA

The painful truth of the destructive power of words hit
home to me in my mid-twenties. Jack and I were hoping to add another little one to our family and we thought the
timing was right. I got pregnant immediately but miscarried
five weeks later. We tried again, and this time I sailed past the
first six weeks without a hitch. However, at seventeen weeks,
I began spotting and my doctor ordered a sonogram. As the
technician scanned my belly, I looked for a little baby on the
screen, but saw nothing. I started panicking and asked, "Where
is the baby?" The technician said she couldn't answer my question. I knew something was terribly wrong, but was hoping
that maybe her screen was malfunctioning … anything but

what I suspected. Finally a doctor entered the room and told me the fetus had died and was so small they could barely see it.

I was devastated, and drove home sobbing and shaking all the way. I was crushed to lose this baby we had wanted with all our hearts. I arrived home and collapsed into Jack's arms as he opened the front door. For our daughter Sarah, unfortunately, this would become her earliest memory: watching her mom sob uncontrollably as her dad tried to comfort her.

Many folks in our community knew I was pregnant because of our positions at the church, and the heartache of losing this baby was compounded in the coming weeks by insensitive comments as the news spread: "The baby was probably deformed anyway. It's best that you lost it." "You're still young; you'll have plenty of children." "My brother's sister-in-law …" followed by a detailed story of a relative's miscarriage. But the harshest comment of all came from a member of our singing group. A week after the miscarriage, I returned to church, still reeling from the loss but needing to take those first tentative steps back toward normalcy. As I knelt to open my guitar case before Mass, a woman called out, "I hear your apple cart tipped!" Wow. My eyes began tearing up and I wasn't sure I could get up off the floor. The combination of raging hormones and a thoughtless comment—perhaps she'd meant to be funny or to lighten the mood—had combined to make that morning one I'll never forget.

What I learned that day is how important words are, particularly when another person is suffering. I now simply say, "I am so sorry" before anything else. What people want more than anything when faced with a loss is just to be comforted and listened to. Look the person in the eye, extend a gentle handshake or hug, and take in the depth of emotion. It is healing to walk right into another's pain and address it, not trying to sugarcoat or explain it away.

Luckily, another young mother in our parish who had also suffered a miscarriage called soon after and asked how I was doing. I relayed to her some of the unkind comments I'd received and she listened patiently. Sharing the hurt made the sting slowly evaporate, and I'll never forget her kindness and sensitivity.

## Putting the Wisdom into Practice

Do you know someone who has suffered a loss recently or is going through a difficult time? Perhaps call or email to say hi, send a gift card to a local cafe or bakery, or invite the person to tea or coffee. Be ready to listen. Your presence will be a great gift. These little gestures *do* make a difference. If you've been there, and felt the care and love of others during a tough time, you know, like I do, the relief and joy knowing we aren't in the dark alone.

# Week Four

If we are to love our neighbors, before doing anything else we must see our neighbors.... We must see not just their faces but the life behind and within their faces. Here it is love that is the frame we see them in.

—FREDERICK BUECHNER

Work is a privilege. It is a participation in creation, an opportunity to make the world more just. Work is where the Creator goes on creating through us.

—SISTER JOAN CHITTISTER

I was a vendor at a national conference in Buffalo, New York, and had a rare two-hour break in the morning schedule. I returned to my hotel room to do some yoga and found an older immigrant woman fluffing up the bed pillows. Disappointed that I wouldn't be alone, I asked if she would mind if I did some yoga while she tidied the room. She smiled and said, "Yes, I would like to see that." I promptly changed clothes and began doing some warm-up stretches.

Trying to break the awkwardness of the situation, I asked the woman, Sitta, a few questions, and we struck up an easy back-and-forth conversation. She told me a bit about her children, and I told her about mine. I mentioned that I teach yoga, and she informed me that her doctor had recently instructed her to begin exercising. She thought yoga would help her relax from the stresses of her job. Sitta watched me do a few lunges, and then asked if I could show her how to do them. Sitta's smile grew larger with every pose she tried, as she listened carefully to the small adjustments I asked her to make. She exclaimed several times, "Ooooo! That feels so good!" After about ten minutes, Sitta returned to her tasks and became my private cheering section, praising my Half Moon and Tree poses. I smiled, enveloped by the warmth of this hardworking sixty-three-year-old woman who had come to the United States in search of a better life for her family.

Sitta carefully folded the last few towels and headed for the door. I apologized that I'd left my wallet at my booth and couldn't give her the customary tip as we said good-bye to each other and she wheeled her cart to the next room.

A few hours later, I saw Sitta perched on a concrete ledge at the hotel entrance, waiting for a bus. "Sitta!" I called out. She smiled and said, "Hello! How was your day?" "Very good!" I replied, reaching into my backpack to retrieve a small bill to press into her hand. It was a small token of gratitude to her, an acknowledgment of the millions of immigrants who serve us daily, often invisibly. As I rode the elevator to my room, I thought of my immigrant great-grandparents who had paved the way for me. Their hard work and courage made my life possible, and now I was benefiting from Sitta's labor, too. What began as disappointment in the lack of solitude for a yoga session was replaced by a delightful encounter, reminding me of my roots and my gratitude to those who toil "behind the scenes."

# Putting the Wisdom into Practice

Keep your eyes open this week for the servants in your life: restaurant workers, cleaning attendants, bellmen, baristas, cashiers, bank tellers. How often we don't even notice them! Give them the gift of recognition. Pause for an extra moment, look them in the eye, address them by name, if possible, and thank them for their service. In this way, you've acknowledged the *person*, not just the "servant."

# LOOKING FORWARD TO NEXT YEAR

I join my hands in thanks for the many wonders of life.
—THICH NHAT HANH

As you begin the next chapter in your journey, I encourage you to revisit the important lessons in life and vow to practice them throughout the coming year. Live with an open heart. Be vulnerable and aware of your imperfections. Connect with others. Remember those who are struggling. Compliment someone. Savor life. Try a new hobby. Take a walk or hike. Listen patiently to others. Stop trying to be perfect. Be grateful *in* difficult situations, not *for* them. Face your fears and work to conquer them. Have a growth mindset. Do the most important task first each day. Write a letter. Notice judgmental thoughts. Cultivate Teflon for criticism, Velcro for compliments. Rejoice in another's joy. Open and close doors carefully and mindfully. Take a deep breath every few hours. Be real and tenderhearted. Find a new way to nurture your creativity. Taste, really taste, your meals. Do chores attentively. Go play. Notice something new. Say thank you. Be kind. Go outside and look at the stars. Tell someone you love them.

# NOTES

## January

1. This wisdom is from an online gratitude course I took years ago with Brother David Steindl-Rast.

## February

1. David Brooks, "The Art of Presence," *New York Times* (January 20, 2014).

## April

1. Lawrence of the Resurrection, *The Practice of the Presence of God,* edited by Conrad De Meester, translated by Salvatore Sciurba (Washington, DC: ICS Publications, 1994), xxxv.

## May

1. Adapted from Bronnie Ware, *The Top Five Regrets of the Dying: A Life Transformed by the Dearly Departing* (Carlsbad, CA: Hay House, 2012).

## June

1. Fred Rogers, commencement speech, Marquette University, Milwaukee, WI, May 29, 2001. Available at www.marquette.edu /commencement/2001/address.html.
2. Margery Williams, *The Velveteen Rabbit* (New York: Doubleday, 1958, 1991), 16–17.
3. Kate Taylor, "The New Case for Women on Corporate Boards: New Perspectives, Increased Profits," *Forbes Magazine* (June 26, 2012).

## August

1. Marcus Borg, *The Heart of Christianity: Rediscovering a Life of Faith* (New York: HarperOne, 2004), 161–62.

2. Gretchen Reynolds, "How Walking in Nature Changes the Brain," *New York Times* (July 22, 2015).

## September

1. Thomas Merton, *Conjectures of a Guilty Bystander* (New York: Image, 1968), 73.
2. Anne Lamott, *Operating Instructions: A Journal of My Son's First Year* (New York: Pantheon, 1992), 214.

## October

1. Kathleen Norris, *Amazing Grace: A Vocabulary of Faith* (New York: Riverhead Books, 1998), 17.

## Additional Weeks to Fill Out the Year

1. Brené Brown, *The Gifts of Imperfection: Let Go of Who You Think You're Supposed to Be and Embrace Who You Are* (Center City, MN: Hazelden, 2010), 73.

# SUGGESTIONS FOR FURTHER READING

Borg, Marcus. *The Heart of Christianity: Rediscovering a Life of Faith*. New York: HarperOne, 2004.

Brown, Brené. *The Gifts of Imperfection: Let Go of Who You Think You're Supposed to Be and Embrace Who You Are*. Center City, MN: Hazelden, 2010.

Chittister, Joan. *Wisdom Distilled from the Daily: Living the Rule of Saint Benedict Today*. New York: HarperCollins, 1990.

Chödrön, Pema. *The Places That Scare You: A Guide to Fearlessness in Difficult Times*. Boston: Shambhala Publications, 2001.

Csikszentmihalyi, Mihaly. *Flow: The Psychology of Optimal Experience*. New York: HarperCollins, 2008.

Duhigg, Charles. *The Power of Habit: Why We Do What We Do in Life and Business*. New York: Random House, 2012.

Hanson, Rick. *Hardwiring Happiness: The New Brain Science of Contentment, Calm and Confidence*. New York: Harmony Books, 2013.

Kondo, Marie. *The Life-Changing Magic of Tidying Up: The Japanese Art of Decluttering and Organizing*. New York: Ten Speed Press, 2014.

Lamott, Anne. *Operating Instructions: A Journal of My Son's First Year*. New York: Pantheon, 1992.

Lawrence of the Resurrection. *The Practice of the Presence of God*. Edited by Conrad De Meester. Translated by Salvatore Sciurba. Washington, DC: ICS Publications, 1994.

Lindahl, Kay. *The Sacred Art of Listening: Forty Reflections for Cultivating a Spiritual Practice*. Woodstock, VT: SkyLight Paths, 2001.

McGee, Margaret D. *Sacred Attention: A Spiritual Practice for Finding God in the Moment*. Woodstock, VT: SkyLight Paths, 2010.

Merton, Thomas. *Conjectures of a Guilty Bystander*. New York: Image, 1968.

Ware, Bronnie. *The Top Five Regrets of the Dying: A Life Transformed by the Dearly Departing*. Carlsbad, CA: Hay House, 2012.

Williams, Margery. *The Velveteen Rabbit*. New York: Doubleday, 1958, 1991.